AF844612

CHINA'S NEW CREATIVE AGE

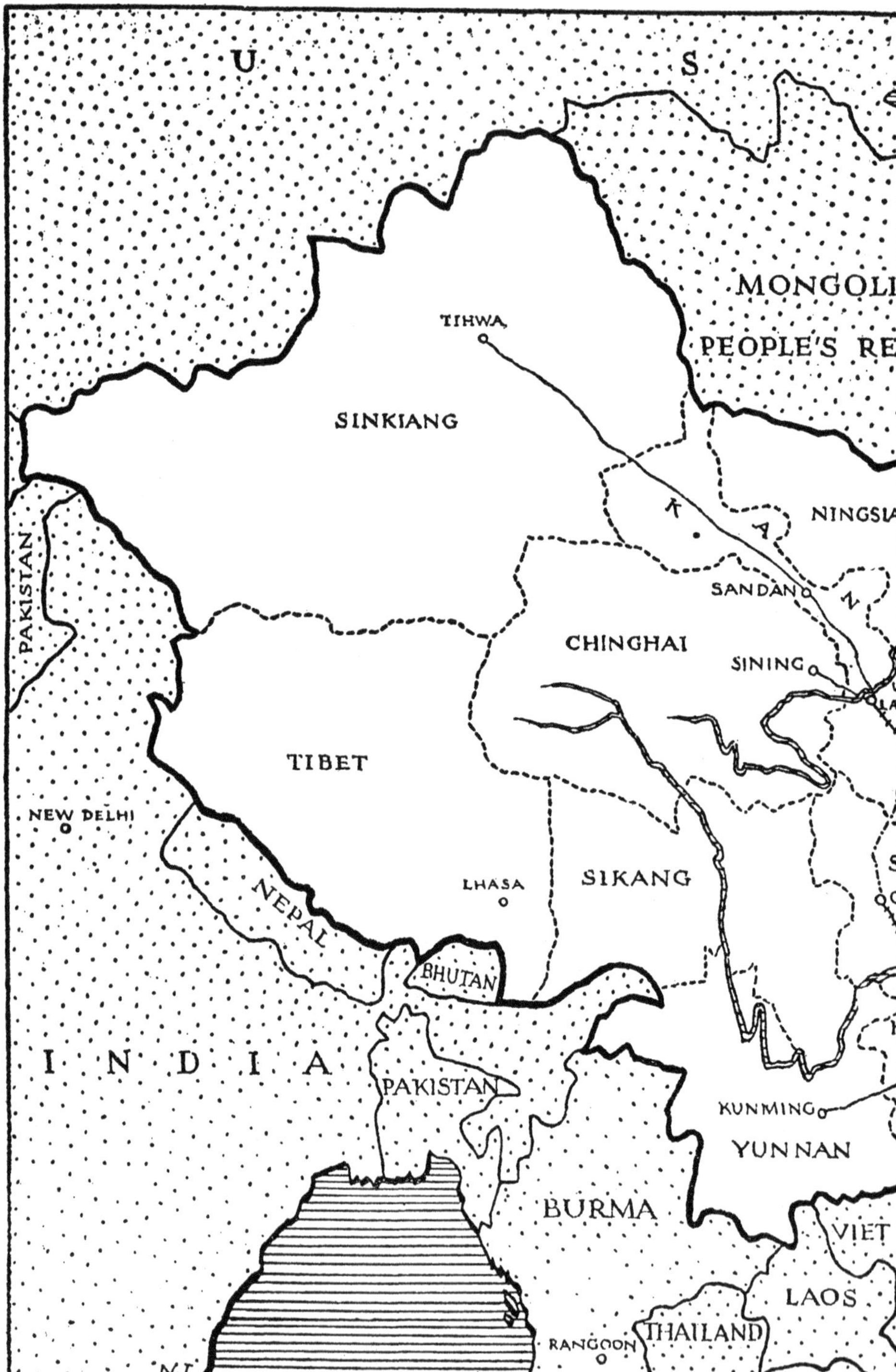
U S
MONGOLI
PEOPLE'S RE
TIHWA
SINKIANG
PAKISTAN
K A N
NINGSIA
SANDAN
CHINGHAI
SINING
TIBET
NEW DELHI
SIKANG
LHASA
NEPAL
BHUTAN
I N D I A
PAKISTAN
KUNMING
YUNNAN
BURMA
VIET
LAOS
THAILAND
RANGOON
N.J.

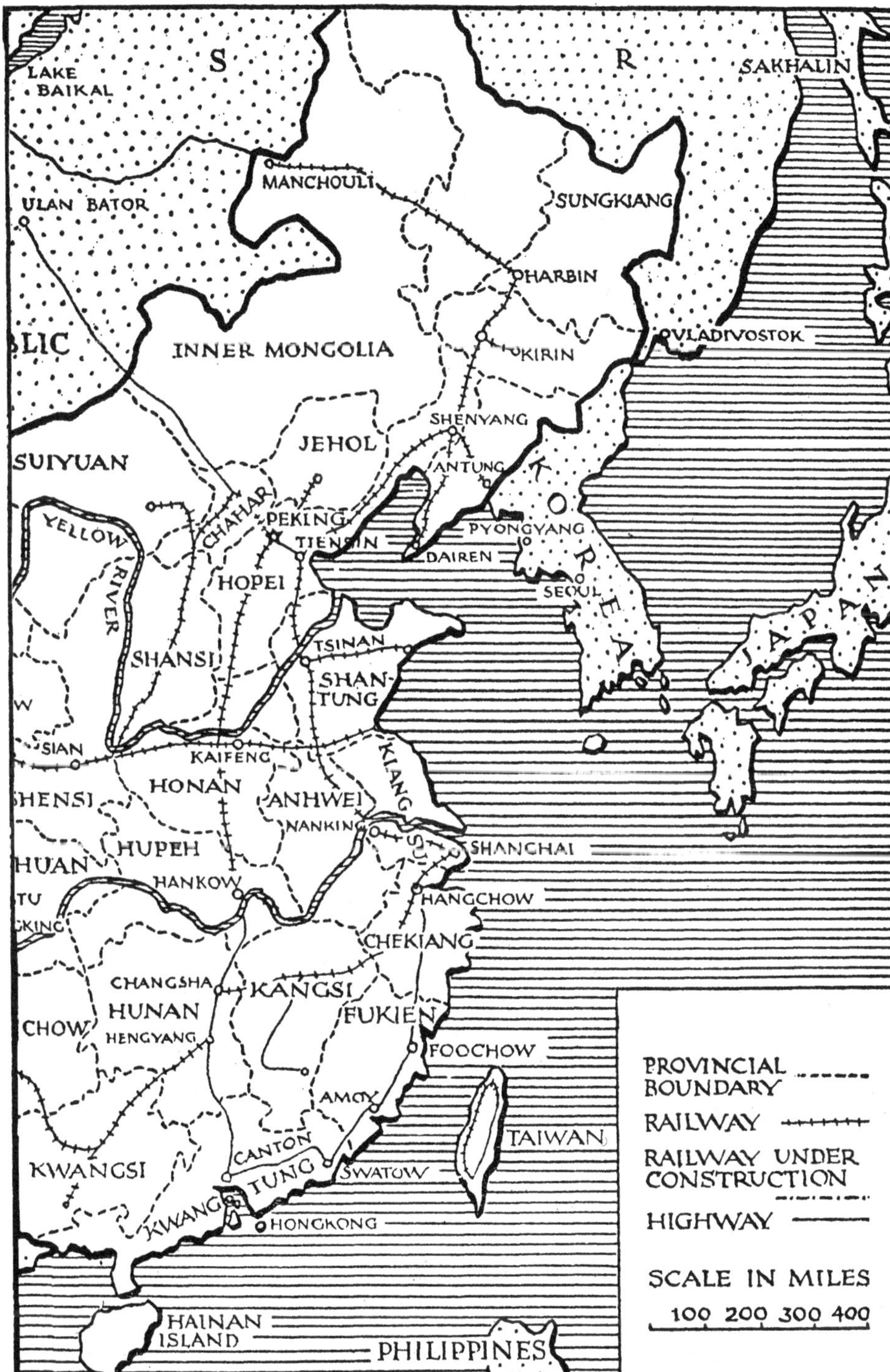

LAKE BAIKAL
S
R
SAKHALIN
MANCHOULI
SUNGKIANG
ULAN BATOR
HARBIN
VLADIVOSTOK
BLIC
INNER MONGOLIA
KIRIN
SHENYANG
JEHOL
SUIYUAN
ANTUNG
KOREA
CHAHAR
PEKING
YELLOW RIVER
TIENTSIN
PYONGYANG
DAIREN
HOPEI
SEOUL
JAPAN
SHANSI
TSINAN
SHANTUNG
SIAN
KAIFENG
KIANGSU
SHENSI
HONAN
ANHWEI
NANKING
HUPEH
SHANGHAI
HUAN
HANKOW
HANGCHOW
CHEKIANG
CHANGSHA
KANGSI
HUNAN
FUKIEN
CHOW
HENGYANG
FOOCHOW
AMOY
TAIWAN
CANTON
KWANGSI
TUNG
SWATOW
KWANG
HONGKONG
HAINAN ISLAND
PHILIPPINES
PROVINCIAL BOUNDARY
RAILWAY
RAILWAY UNDER CONSTRUCTION
HIGHWAY
SCALE IN MILES
100 200 300 400

China's New Creative Age

By Hewlett Johnson

Dean of Canterbury

with drawings and maps by

NOWELL JOHNSON

GREENWOOD PRESS, PUBLISHERS
WESTPORT, CONNECTICUT

The Library of Congress has catalogued this publication as follows:

Library of Congress Cataloging in Publication Data

Johnson, Hewlett, 1874-1966.
China's new creative age.

Reprint of the 1953 ed.
1. China (People's Republic of China, 1949-)--Social conditions. 2. China (People's Republic of China, 1949-)--Economic conditions. 3. China (People's Republic of China, 1949-)--Politics and government. I. Title.
[DS777.55.J64 1973] 915.1'03'5 72-11477
ISBN 0-8371-6671-3

Copyright 1953 by International Publishers Co., Inc.

Originally published in 1953
by International Publishers, New York

Reprinted with the permission
of International Publishers

First Greenwood Reprinting 1973

Library of Congress Catalogue Card Number 72-11477

ISBN 0-8371-6671-3

Printed in the United States of America

CONTENTS

LIST OF ILLUSTRATIONS

Preface

I WAS THERE is the dramatic title chosen by Admiral Leahey for the book in which he enumerates the memorable journeys of Roosevelt's wartime years. "I was there" might well have been taken as the title of this present book, which relates, in vividly contrasting pictures, the story of two of the widest journeys an ordinary Englishman ever made in this vast land of China, peopled by a quarter or more of the world's population.

"I was there," north, south, east and west; in China's European-dominated coastal towns; in her own capital towns, ancient and modern, of Peking and Nanking; in Hankow, the Chicago of the Central Lands; and then on and beyond the Great Wall, into Inner Mongolia in the deep north and on beyond Kansu into Tibet in the deep west, in the year 1932, when China groaned under the blows of enemies external and internal; savage blows from Japan, and treacherous blows from the Kuomintang; when the tillers of the land writhed under exactions of feudal landlords and extortionate taxation; when women were serfs to husbands and state; when graft went hand in hand with poverty, ignorance and disease; when the land was submerged by floods or parched by drought, and when disbanded armies filled the country-side with bandits and life with terror.

And then, in vivid, never-to-be-forgotten contrast "I was there" in 1952, when the new creative China had risen from the ground, had scattered her enemies, had smashed her fetters and was standing on her feet and unbound, ready to assume her rightful place in what Professor Arnold Toynbee "feels" will be the new center of power in the coming centuries—the East.

"I was there" when Japan had been vanquished and the Kuomintang expelled, when the terror of feudalism lived on only as a hideous dream of the past; when the men who tilled the land owned the land; when women took their rightful place as equals side by side with men; when rivers in flood were progressively tamed and forced in drought to irrigate the land; when graft, poverty and banditry were relentlessly assailed and with them ignorance, dirt and disease; when a new morality was prevailing and new hopes set new smiles on faces young and old; when the new creative China was emerging as a foremost champion of world peace, and together with all Russia and all Eastern Europe, was bringing the world with giant strides nearer to the days of universal brotherhood.

"He is mad," said Venice of Marco Polo in the latter half of the thirteenth century when he had visited and had returned from China. He had gone, he had seen, he was enthralled. Enthralled by the wonder of Chinese towns and palaces with their glory of space and proportion, with their marble balustrades and glazed and colored roofs, with their gay streets and silken banners, with their thronged canals, teeming with junks and spanned by a thousand graceful bridges. After his journeys of four years through seven thousand miles of travel each way, and after his long sojourn in Cathay, Marco Polo was home again in Venice speaking to all who would listen of the wonderlands on the far side of the world.

"He is mad," they said.

We too have been to China, but in the mid-twentieth century. By plane, not caravan: in days, not years. We have traveled thither seven thousand miles each way at a speed utterly unknown in Polo's days, and then seven thousand miles, in seven weeks intensive tour and study through the length and breadth of China, a land as large as Europe and twice as populous.

We too went, we saw, we were enthralled. Enthralled by the same beauties that had enthralled Marco Polo, beauties of temples and palaces, fashioned on eternal lines, products of millennia of cultured tradition, akin in spirit to the Grecian temples in Athens or to the Moslem mosques in Samarkand.

But on and beyond all that, which indeed I had seen and loved in 1932, we were enthalled and conquered in this second journey by something that Marco Polo never saw. By a new creative beauty, a new liberation of manhood and womanhood; by the mastery, and compelled ministry, of nature's forces; by the shining glance of China's new youth, boys and girls; by the beauty of vast moral changes, by her new way of living, and by the beauty of a purpose providing scope for every man, woman and child to be themselves, to be what the gods meant them to be, willing agents in the task of building a new human complexity, compact with infinite human variety and issuing in the release of latent and unexpected human qualities.

Doubtless, too, many will say of us, no less than of Marco Polo: "They are mad." But whereas it took centuries to verify the truth of Polo's tales, it will not, I venture to suggest, take centuries to verify the truth of ours. A bare three years have passed since liberation day and the points on the graph of change strike so steep a curve as will speedily astonish a hostile war-like world and spread deep confidence among all peace-loving peoples.

A thousand difficulties and dangers still remain. China has a long way yet to go. Powerful enemies threaten her from without and seek to disrupt her from within. Vast deficiencies still on the material side, and evil strands of character on the moral side still cripple her. But a radical change of direction has set her upon a new path to a new goal, along which she travels at startling speed.

The story of that change and speedy advance, with examination of those dangers and difficulties, form the theme of this book.

PART I. THE PEOPLE'S VICTORY

1 China's Human Enemies Defeated

THE WHITE-HAIRED GIRL

CHINA produces her own drama, her own opera, her own films; not crude, raw productions, but finished, polished and competent. Learning admirably as to form from the Western world—as, for example, in music, where she lagged behind the West—she provides her own vital new content, skillfully blending new with old, never descending to vulgarities and never losing her traditional genius, handed down from generation to generation through the long centuries.

Twenty years ago I saw the old Chinese drama in village and city. Today I see it anew, westernized in its music, westernized in its realistic technique, suffering no loss of Chinese subtlety and charm in the process, but now shot through and through with the fire of Chinese "liberation" passion born of the national struggle for the new Chinese order.

A striking example is the film *The White-Haired Girl,* which, while inspiring and educating the Chinese masses for whom it was written and out of whose experience it grew, now travels far and wide through the peace-loving world. We had heard of its moving beauty in London, in Prague, and in Moscow; we witnessed it ourselves in Peking, and, as it rings so true to the great realities which it unfolds, its brief recital will make an appropriate introduction to ampler descriptions of the logic and nature of the radical changes in the new China.

Based possibly on legend, but true as are all great legends, the story has grown from a simple recital in prose or verse to a polished dramatic whole, till now it stands, like a Greek epic or like our English Robin Hood, an intrinsic part of the people's art, something of their very flesh and blood. In it we hear the people speak to themselves. They are the authors, the actors and the audience. As the film moves to its dénouement the audience murmurs louder and ever louder in sympathy and recognition. For China, it epitomizes the story of a thousand years of feudal exploitation broken by the rising of a people's will.

The film opens with a scene of idyllic beauty. An old peasant shepherd sings as he leads his sheep from pasture to pasture on the mountain side. The view is lovely but the song sad: the shepherd sings of the sorrows of his land.

That is the overture. It is followed by a vivid contrast, the contrast between cruel and heedless wealth and grinding poverty. The full consequences of this are normally hidden in capitalist societies; they were open and bare and blatant with the Chinese feudal landlords.

A landlord reclines on a sultry summer day on a chaise-longue in the rich man's room of a country mansion. One obsequious servant fans his face, another gently massages his limbs. . . . A swift transition takes us to the tenants' fields, among the villagers, reaping maize in the sweltering sun, stopping now and then to straighten the back and wipe the sweat off the steaming brow. Old men and women, young men and girls toil on in the blazing heat.

An old man calls to his daughter, a beautiful girl, half hidden in the maize: "Work less hard, child." But work hard she knows she must. The debts of a bad season threaten her father and she has certain longings for herself.

At midday an old woman brings broth for the workers. They sit in the shade and eat. After some chaff from the old folks, a handsome lad and the beautiful girl wander off alone and a charming love scene ensues.

The struggle to meet the exorbitant rent and debt repayments to the landlord intermingles now with the struggle to buy the young couple a home. Long and dangerous toil follows. The girl lowers the boy down the cliff face to procure fuel salable in this timber-starved land. Bitter is the talk on the threshing floor as the landlord's huge proportion is measured out and the pitiful remainder displayed, the workers' only reward for a year's hard toil.

At length, however, money is saved, a home procured, and the lovers prepare for their bridal day.

The landlord has other ideas; driving luxuriously past the weary peasants, he cast lascivious eyes on the girl, and when the old man fails to meet new and deliberately impossible exactions, he turns a deaf ear to every plea for patience and demands, "Sell your daughter."

The father recoils in horror. Falls on his knees. Implores pity. Despite his cries and remonstrances, the bailiff completes the bill of sale, drags the old man to the table, covers his thumb with ink and presses it on the foot of the deed. The girl is sold.

The old man's utter misery provides perhaps the most poignant moment of the film and is acted with transcendent skill. Then comes the eve of the New Year's Day feast. The father sits silent. He refuses food. His daughter falls asleep on his shoulder. He puts her gently to rest on the low couch, kisses her brow, brushes aside his flooding tears and staggers out into the snow of the bitter night. Looking this way and that, he finds no way of escape save in the poison, which he drinks, and throws himself down to die on the threshold of the landlord's house.

At dawn the neighbors find his body. The daughter flings herself upon him, refusing to acknowledge death. It is an agonizing scene, culminating in the arrival of the landlord's bailiff to demand the girl in redemption of the bond. The horrified relatives, young and old, plead in vain. The bailiff exhibits the bond and the signature. They prepare to resist. But the bailiff's armed guard seize the girl and drag her struggling to the landlord's house. In utter misery she resists all his advances.

The elderly maid of the landlord's old mother pities the child and takes her to the old woman, a selfish, cruel Buddhist devotee who insists on having the girl as her attendant. For the moment the girl is saved from violation; instead, she is subjected daily to cruel humiliations from the old woman.

The landlord, however, steals at dusk one evening into the room where the girl stands alone trimming the lamp on the Buddhist altar. He overpowers her and violates her.

She is only saved from self-destruction by the old serving-woman. Together they plan an escape with the girl's lover. The plot is discovered and foiled. The lad flees from the guns. The girl returns to her living death.

Earlier in the film an old man had told the lovers of the wonders of the Red Army, which was holding out in the fastnesses of the mountains of Shensi, resisting alone the Japanese invaders. The boy seeks to join them, and we follow his long struggles, crowned with success, as with splendid photography we see two strong hands—nothing more—stretch down the cliff face to seize and draw him to safety. He is at last with the men "with the Red Star" on their caps, the sign he was to seek.

He becomes leader of a detachment and at length advances to his own village to administer the new land-distribution law.

In the meantime, the girl, now pregnant, learns that she is to be sold as a slave. For the landlord is to be married, and his mother declares, "We cannot have a pregnant girl in the house on my son's marriage day." The old serving-woman urges flight, thrusts all her savings into the girl's hands, and pushes her forth into the night.

Escaping pursuit, the fugitive takes refuge in a dripping cave high up on the mountainside, far from the haunts of men and among terrifying wild beasts. There, in a scene marked by exquisite delicacy and restraint, she gives birth to her child. It dies. Her hair turns white.

For food she gathers berries, eking them out with bread taken by stealth from the altar of a lonely Buddhist temple. And there one night she terrifies the landlord and his steward, who had come in for refuge from a thunderstorm. They see her white hair lit up by a flash of lightning. And she, too, sees the faces of her bitterest enemies. She hurls a heavy temple bronze at them as they hurry in terror away, and sees them tumble down the face of the cliff.

Escaping death, however, they reach home—where they hear that the advance guard of the Red Army has come and will enforce the new land laws, as was their wont in occupied territory.

The landlord, alarmed by his impending losses, plots with his bailiff a delaying action. They set fire to one of the village houses, and stick up outside a notice saying that the fire was caused by the white-haired witch in the mountains.

The young cadre and his men, to probe the tale, set off to search the mountain. They see the girl and fire at her. She scrambles up to her cave in the rocks. Pausing breathless on the threshold, she peers down to watch her pursuers. She sees and recognizes her betrothed. Half-fainting and utterly exhausted, she calls his name.

Springing to her side he seizes her as she totters to fall. Brushing the white hair aside, he recognizes her face and smooths it gently as she swoons.

Then comes the day of judgment, when the tenants, massed around the judges' table, lay innumerable and horrible charges agianst the landlord. Dramatically the white-haired girl appears and confronts him.

With fury in their eyes, the tenants rush upon the landlord to slay him there and then. The young officer holds them back. Things must be done in order and by law. The case proceeds. The landlord, guilty of many crimes, is condemned to death. His armorial bearings over the manor-house are torn down and burned, together with all the bonds which held the tenants in servitude.

The story is essentially, if not literally, true. Landlords' luxury at the expense of peasant poverty was true. Servitude of workers was true. Bondage of womanhood was true. Landlords' lasciviousness and purchase of girls was true. The sale of young girls to meet impossible debt was true. Cruelty and ruthlessness were true.

So, too, was peasant deliverance by the Red Army true. Mass trials

New hopes set new smiles on faces young and old.

were true. Insistence upon legally correct procedure at trials was true. Division of land was true. And most true of all was the rejoicing at the new liberation.

THE END OF FEUDAL CHINA

One of the most interesting foreigners to visit China and to take up his abode there is Rewi Alley, a name more familiar in Australia and America than here. This powerfully-built New Zealander, with strong, rough-cut face and sandy hair reminiscent of the Scottish Highlanders I knew in my youth, coming from a scholastic family, had served as a factory inspector in Shanghai under the Kuomintang until, sickened by the cruel brutality of the foreign factory-owners even to children of tenderest years, he had shaken the dust of their factories from off his feet and had gone to Szechuan to train Chinese youth to run their own industry, beginning with small units, which were built up by co-operative efforts. It was a movement of much promise.

Obstructed perpetually by the Kuomintang officials, Alley moved further and further westward and northward, until at length he was driven to the westernmost valleys of Kanzu, the country I knew so well in 1932. There at the small town of Sandan he had created a highly successful Chinese co-operative industrial center, which has now expanded, and operates in coal, oil, weaving, and pottery. A charming glazed figure of a small child, which now looks a Tang horse in the face on my Deanery table, though a thousand years separate the two, came as a gift from his factory. Some of Alley's pupils, having received an elementary technical training as doctors and surgeons from Robert Spencer, a highly competent English surgeon, who worked voluntarily for many years at the same center, now practice even the new "skin-tissue" treatment of which I shall speak in a later chapter.

Alley works on with full encouragement from the Liberation Government. By good fortune, he happened to be in Peking at the time of our arrival and enabled me to piece together the story of the changes which had taken place since we missed one another by three days twenty years ago.

In his presence, one evening, I happened to talk of a land-divided village, several miles from Peking, where we had spent the day, studying conditions, visiting farms and buildings and schools, and discussing with men, women, and children their new life and hopes. Overhearing my casual remark that the village we had examined was doubtless somewhat exceptional—a mistake I was later able to rectify myself—Alley had broken in: "Not at all. Do you remember such-and-such places in Kanzu?" I did. "Do you remember how derelict the villages were, and how listless the air of the peasants, how they were just letting things slide?" I did; and I recollected too that Major Todd, my American engineering friend, with whom I had traveled to Kanzu, had put this desolation down to the wreckage caused by the Moslem-Chinese wars, which had swept to and fro over western Kanzu. We had just left it at that. We were wrong: it was in the main the fruit of local tyranny.

"Well," said Alley, "you would scarcely recognize those places today. Everything is transformed. The villages are transformed. The people are transformed. The countryside is transformed. The land is cultivated as never before. Old women with bound and hobbled feet, who never in their lives had touched pick and spade or hoe, now help men and youth in the fields. Not a patch is left untended. The land thrives. The village thrives. It is pleasant to handle one's own harvest, no longer claimed by a landlord."

"Why?"

"Because the landlords and landladies have gone. Publicly tried, and legally sentenced, they have been removed and their land has been divided among the peasants."

The trials at mass meetings at which the local population had given evidence had revealed facts utterly unknown to foreigners and strangers, even to Alley, who had spent twenty-five years in China and had lived for long years outside the castellated walls of the local magnates, behind which these devilish crimes had been committed.

Alley recalled three local trials and specified the deeds revealed and acknowledged at impressive mass trial meetings, conducted with all the punctilious legalities and safeguards which we had noted in the trial scenes of *The White-Haired Girl*.

Case 1. An old landlady had confessed to seven direct murders. With her own hands she had smothered her son's wife in bed. With her own hands she had poured boiling gruel over her slave girl till death ended the child's suffering. By her own fiat she had summoned to her home people unable to repay loans and had had them killed there.

Case 2. A landlord, whose benign appearance belied a vicious and cruel character, had insisted on his rights as a landlord to practice the "first night" with every village bride. And that while he suffered from a venereal disease, with which he had infected them.

Case 3. Most ruthless and horrible of all, and unbelievable in its dénouement, was the case of a third landlord. Disliking a certain family, he determined to liquidate them all. He killed fourteen of them. Then he learned that a small baby grandchild, the last of the whole family, was hidden in a distant village. He discovered the "hide-out" and went there. He was a big man and strong, weighing 220 pounds. He took the baby by the two legs and literally tore it asunder. He dared not deny the deed; at the public trial he said: "Yes, I did it."

Pleasant to handle one's own harvest, no longer claimed by a landlo.d.

The removal of these vicious local landed proprietors had lifted an intolerable load from off men's minds. The whole attitude and spirit of the village had changed. Now the land was the villagers' land. The village was free. Men and women were debt-free. Young girls and brides were inviolate. Inhibiting fears had gone. Creative energy was released. The villages had begun at once to thrive. The land had blossomed. Prosperity had replaced poverty. A new era had dawned.

Some day I hope to return to that land of western Kanzu, whose fruitful and flowering valleys lie 5,000 feet above sea-level, with snow-clad heights beyond, places known to few Englishmen, but crammed with historic interest—the fascinating land, where Professor Joseph Needham, the Cambridge biologist, whom we met in Peking, has spent long holidays with Rewi Alley—whom he catalogues as "one of the half-dozen men in whom it has been possible to see and touch that which constitutes human greatness"—preparing his monumental book on ancient Chinese hydraulic engineering and water control.

I have singled out Rewi Alley's lurid tales* because they deal with a locality I know. But what happened there has happened in varying degrees in countless other districts and villages throughout the whole of the vast land of China. These were not exceptional events. I could multiply such instances indefinitely. But there is no need. It has already been done and amply done. Jack Belden, the American writer, who cannot be accused of propaganda in favor of communism nor of exaggeration as a journalist, relates in his book, *China Shakes the World,* and at nauseating and even tedious length, similar stories, straight, like these, from the lips of the men and women involved; and he culls his stories from widely separated areas of China.

He relates, for instance, how in one village, while he was there, twenty-four bodies, including women and children, were exhumed from a common pit where they had been buried alive and then partially uncovered and eaten by dogs. Landlords, he says, very often buried alive men who had engaged in the struggle for reduction of rents. If they could not find these men, they buried their families. He gives an appalling picture of men buried up to the neck, their eyes starting from their heads, but still alive, left to slow death, undefended against ravages of insects or dogs.

The power of the landlords ranged not only over the lives of the men, but over the bodies of their womankind. Landlords could, in general, have whatever relations they pleased with the wives of their tenants and, as we saw in *The White-Haired Girl,* with their tenants' daughters. A rich peasant or landlord would wait until a farmer was in the field, and then visit the house and deal as he liked with the wife. There was small chance of redress. The landlord had his armed guards, and his or his bailiff's henchmen were, as often as not, the only village government officials—with control also of the police, to whom the man could appeal.

* Rewi Alley has happily published a series of diaries, and almost contemporary with this book an excellent volume called *Yo Banfa!* (*We Have a Way*) which is vivid with first-hand experience of more than twenty years in China. This book is published by *China Monthly Review,* Shanghai, 1952.

The institution of slave girls, concubinage, and forced marriage was inseparable from the Chinese feudal landlord system. Slave girls were drudges in the landlord's house, used as concubines by his sons or sold to merchants, who shipped them to Shanghai where they were forced into prostitution or compelled to enter factories. Jack Belden relates how, with his own eyes, in various Kuomintang Army headquarters, he had seen officers call in the local gentry and ask their aid in securing young girls for their use as long as they were in the territory: virgin daughters of poor tenant farmers were the popular choice.

Naturally, not all landlords were bad, and when bad there were degrees of badness. But the general picture, as it has now been unfolded in the innumerable trials that have taken place, tells a tale which, happily, is at last, and after 2,000 years of struggle, ended.

Even where physical cruelty was absent, the cruelty of exorbitant usury was of frequent occurrence and disastrous in its consequences. A farmer, for instance, had borrowed 100 *catties* (130 lbs.) of millet before planting, to be paid back at harvest time by 200 *catties*. Failure to pay raised the interest to 300 *catties*, the next year. Unable even then to repay the loan because of drought, he was obliged to sell 4 *mou* of his land (1 *mou* =0.16 acre), leaving soil insufficient to support his family. His mother and two children starved to death.

"Why," I asked Rewi Alley, "did not the missionaries tell us of these things and enlist our sympathy in the fight against them?"

"Because," he said, "the missionaries aimed, as a matter of policy, at converting the middle-class Chinese. They paid less attention to the poorer peasants or to the landlords, from whom, perhaps, they received aid and privileges."

I might also add that many missionaries would doubtless have known even less than Rewi Alley what went on behind those castellated walls. The native Chinese had always entertained a certain suspicion of missionaries from foreign imperialist lands, a suspicion which grew rapidly when they saw the United States aiding the Kuomintang and its dominant clique.

This monstrous feudal land system, now swept so peremptorily and speedily away, has had a history of 2,500 years behind it. No wonder the peasants regard with awe, veneration, and deep affection the Red Army, which has rid them forever of landlord tyranny. Mao Tse-tung has consummated in so short a time and in so effective and conclusive a manner a struggle which had begun far back in history in the revolt of 209 B.C., followed all down the ages by hundreds of other revolts, all ineffective and all in their time ending in disaster and bitter disappointment.

Not even had the most massive and long-drawn-out revolt of all—the Taiping rebellion—succeeded, though it took thirty years of bloody civil war and the aid of foreign arms and foreign troops to quell it. No bourgeois leader had dared to give a lead to the leaderless peasants who had raised the Taiping revolt and waged the Taiping war.

The Taiping revolt was subsequently followed by the Kuomintang revolt, which at first promised fair, but had ended by doing nothing or worse than nothing. For while it had talked of betterment, the lot of the peasants went from bad to worse. The peasant's landstrip grew narrower. What once were public lands became private lands, private gentry seizing the acres which had formerly been devoted to temple and educational purposes. Farming also—a most important point—remained primitive. Large ownership of land had not meant large-scale farming in China, as it had even in tsarist Russia. The Chinese landlord let his land out in small parcels to small tenants and simply lived on the rent. The import of cheap machine-made Western goods made it still harder for the tenant to eke out a living after paying exorbitant rent, since it prevented his wife and daughter from adding, through homecraft, to the impossibly inadequate income from their tiny holding.

The peasant was thus ripe for revolt when Dr. Sun Yat-sen, father of the Kuomintang, co-operating at first with the Communists, realized that without a program of "land to the tiller" they could never overthrow the northern warlords.

Inspired by that program, the peasants, pouring into the Kuomintang Army, had swept Chiang Kai-shek into power.

But the peasants were again betrayed. Tied up with the landlords themselves, the Kuomintang bourgeoisie, with Chiang Kai-shek at their head, betrayed the people. Tu Yush-sen's vicious green gang, acting with Chiang's authority, mowed down the workers of Shanghai. The higher Army officers, most of them large landowners themselves, did not reduce rents by 25 percent as they had promised, but increased them steeply, with threats of dungeons if protest was made.

After the Japanese War, land had become concentrated to an unheard-of degree in ever fewer hands; concentrated so ruthlessly that while, after the war, millions of farmers died of starvation through lack of land, millions of acres were left desolate through lack of farmers. Men, women, and children literally starved to death. Tenant farmers were chained to a plot insufficient to maintain a family. It meant death, for there was no industry or large-scale farming which could employ them as laborers. These poor, starving farmers sought deliverance in vain from the Kuomintang. The day of peasant explosion drew near.

Two results followed. First, the power of Chiang Kai-shek was slowly undermined. Second, the door was open for the Communist leaders to head a peasant revolt. In the graphic words of Jack Belden: "This simple man [the peasant], born to tenant, feudal slavery, to an overworked and crowded plot of ground, stunned into obedience beneath the grasping landlord's hand, dispossessed from his land by crooked deals and savage violence, robbed of his wife's caresses and his children's laughter, suddenly rose with an impassioned thrill and, under the threat of death itself, began to demand land and revenge."

Land reform became the keynote of Communist policy. It gave the peasant hope and handed him a weapon in the struggle with his feudal village lord. Communist leaders had, in this culminating epoch, acted from the first with consummate skill. They drew the people *en masse* into the struggle.

After the kidnapping of Chiang Kai-shek in 1934 and the creation of a united Communist-Kuomintang front against the Japanese, the Communists had, however, called a halt to the peasants' demand for immediate division of land. In that united front period they had preached and practiced rent control as a halfway house to their ultimate goal, and had then carried into effect the Kuomintang promises of 1926 by cutting all rents in the areas they controlled by 25 percent, thus maintaining the necessary unity to carry forward the revolt against the Japanese to a successful conclusion.

At the same time they had unceasingly encouraged the peasants to dare to meet together and air their "bitterness" to one another; in this way drawing peasants out of isolation from one another and creating the groundwork of really democratic institutions and democratic action. Accusation Meetings, Speak Bitterness Meetings, Struggle Meetings became the chief organs of the Chinese Revolution. The individualist peasant began to identify himself with others.

The final defeat of the Japanese had led to a new situation. What was to be the policy now: continued contentment with rent control or drastic land redivision? The decision was urgent. Chiang Kai-shek was battering at the door of the border regions.

There was one immediate step to take, and it was taken. None could complain if the pro-Japanese landlords' acres were seized and divided. Settlement meetings were organized and traitor landlords arraigned, often with understandable violence, but, generally, since the Chinese are a reasonable people, in a more orderly way, without destruction of property and without robbing the evicted landlords of all means of livelihood or loss of personal property.

The immediate result of the division of the traitors' lands, when agricultural output in the liberated areas rose by 50 percent, was apparent to all and hastened on the final decision which was made in the summer of 1946, when the word went forth: "Divide the land!"

That was the beginning of the end of 2,000 years of feudalism in China.

It solved the problem: Who was to rule China? Mao Tse-tung had often asserted that the Party which solved the land question would rule China. He declared that if the Communist policy on land was right, it would win the war both against Japanese invaders and Kuomintang reactionaries. It did both, and much more besides. It settled the problem, for example, of authority in the villages. It released the emotional passion of the peasants. It united the peasants against the Kuomintang which had supported the landlords, but also against the American millionaires who had supported Chiang Kai-shek. It eliminated the reign of the corrupt gentry and set free the money needed to feed the army and fortify the dykes against flood. It broke down many age-old superstitions and the belief that it was fate and not extortionate landlords that had kept the people poor. It was the crucial step into China's New Creative Age.

THE LAND TO THE TILLER

In May, 1946, the Chinese Communist Party decided to change their interim rent and interest reduction policy to the outstandingly radical policy of confiscating estates and redistributing the land to the peasants: the most momentous decision, perhaps, in the whole course of Chinese history.

In June, 1950, eight months after its foundation, the Central People's Government promulgated the new *Land Reform Law,* to be followed, in the same year, by the *Decisions Concerning Differentiation of Class Status in the Countryside.*

These two enactments covered the nationwide campaign to replace

Eagerly listening teen-age boys out of the corner of whose...jackets poked the glittering shafts of fountain pens.

feudalism by peasant ownership in a land twice the size of Western Europe, setting free a farming population greater than that of all Western Europe combined, making 300 million tillers of the land the owners of the land they tilled, lining with new money millions of empty pockets, enabling millions of peasants to build houses, purchase furniture, clothes, pots, pans, kettles and bicycles and providing our engineers and chemists, if they will, with unlimited markets for agricultural machinery and chemical fertilizers.

Visiting an outlying farm in the Pengpu district of the Huai River, we talked with an eager group of peasant farmers. It was an area which had been completely submerged in the great flood of 1950, with widespread destruction of property. Yet here we were, in the summer of 1952, in a village growing ever more thriving, listening to the peasants' tales of the Red Army's approach and the new order of life which followed it.

My eyes wandered as they spoke and alighted on a sight more eloquent than all words. Standing on the outskirts of the village group were three eagerly listening teen-age boys, out of the pockets of whose blue cotton jackets poked the glittering shafts of fountain pens. Teen-agers with fountain pens in a peasant village, and only two years after devastating floods! The thing was incredible and revealing.

Multiply the spending power of that village by China's 300 million rural population, a number half as big again as the total population of Western Europe from Finland to Spain, and you get a picture of trading possibilities in a peaceful world. Fountain pens in peasants' pockets! Small things speak loud in China today.

Incidentally, those fountain pens were Chinese-made and excellent in quality. Chinese shops and bazaars abound in them.

Examining the nature of the land reform which has proceeded with such thoroughness and such lightning speed right across this vast land and was already completed in the main by March, 1951, we first note that two main classes constituted the old village society of China—landlords and peasants.

The landlords were a small, non-working minority, whose holdings were tilled by others, who charged exorbitant rents, who lent money at usury, who hoarded and speculated in grain and as often as not were tax collectors and stole the State tax funds. Too indolent or ignorant to farm on a big scale, their estates were as uneconomic nationally as any small isolated peasant holdings—less economic indeed, because a peasant owner will produce more from his land than a tenant farmer.

Yet this small landlord class, though only 5 percent of the rural population of China, owned between 50 and 60 percent of all agricultural land in the country; 95 percent of the rural population owned less than half of all the land.

The peasant class comprised four groups, as follows:

1. *Rich Peasants.* A well-to-do minority of some 5 percent, who owned a substantial parcel of land with its necessary equipment; working themselves, they hired labor on a long-term basis. Many of them rented out some of their land and also lent money at interest. Rich peasants owned some 10 percent of China's arable land.

2. *Middle Peasants.* A dwindling group who tilled their parcels of land themselves and found difficulty in making ends meet.

3. *Poor Peasants.* This, the biggest group, which had also been growing rapidly, tilled parcels of land too small for subsistence, and lacked the implements to work them. Eking out subsistence as day laborers, these poor peasants lived in semi-starvation, burdened by ever-increasing rents, interest, and debts: comprising half the number of households in a typical village, they possessed only 18 percent of the land.

As tenants, these poor peasants were supposed to pay 40 to 50 percent of the value of their crops as rent. Actually, the rent generally amounted to 60 to 70 percent, because the landlords assessed it on the basis of average area yield, buildings and roads being counted as productive land. There were further exactions. The peasant was often forced, for example, to pay his rent before the harvest, and to do this he must beg a loan from the landlord with interest up to 75 percent.

4. *Hired Laborers.* These were the most miserable of all, sweating year in year out for others, with never a chance of improving their lot. They comprised at the Liberation census about 30 percent of all households in the villages. Pitifully exploited in a multiplicity of ways, they worked from dawn to dusk for a pittance. Often they reached the year's end with no cash at all, not even with enough money to renew their clothing.

Naturally then, it was the poor peasants and the laborers who formed the backbone of the agrarian movement which has at length transformed the whole of China's economy. For land hunger was the key to revolution. Land hunger penetrated the city as well as the country. Families in Chinese towns, large or small, have numerous property contacts with the countryside. Many landlords were absentees in the towns and many poor townspeople are country born and still land hungry. They only seek a temporary livelihood in the city. Bureaus for clarifying titles therefore were needed, both in country and in town.

Land hunger is a passionate thing. I well remember our "batman" when I traveled to Tibet with Major Todd; a townsman of Shanghai, the batman was consumed with a constant passion to buy a small holding of land for himself: he was proportionately grateful when we added to his fund of savings. A man typical of multitudes of townsfolk.

The struggle was on and the battle for the land was fierce. The landlords had allies. The whole weight of foreign influence was on their side. The big battalions of poor peasants and hired laborers, however, were on the attacking side and, led with skill by the Communist Party, they carried to successful conclusion the fight to eliminate the landlord class with astonishing thoroughness, speed, and effectiveness.

The transition was rendered the more possible after the Communist Party had produced stable conditions of government with a trained personnel for planned leadership. Armed bands of reactionary landlords were rounded up. Rural despots removed. Peasant associations reorganized the village administrations. The people gained experience in enforcing their will on former oppressors.

The land reform workers from city and countryside, cooperating with the Peasants' Associations, generally carried the radical reform through in several stages.

1. An exhaustive study is made of a whole administrative area called a *hsiang*, comprising many villages. The study is then extended more intensively to a typical village within it. Jointly city workers and country workers and Peasants' Association delegates explain the government's policy to the people. Accusation Meetings are held. Landlord abuses are brought to light. All to frequently it is discovered that the landlord's property is in the main the people's own property, wrested from them by fraud and violence. The Peasants' Associations are purged of landlords' agents. The long-suppressed popular indignation finds a voice at last. People's Tribunals are set up. Landlords guilty of serious crimes are tried and punished; their prestige disappears; they lose control.

2. The beneficiaries of the reform are thus separated from those who are its target—the landlords. These beneficiaries are then classified into one or other of the categories which will receive the redistributed land. It is open to anyone, landlord or others, to appeal against the decision which places them in this category or that.

Decisions are referred to the sub-county people's government for approval and official announcement. The new class status of every family is thus finally established.

Classification is made flexible within certain limits. Red Army men, or professional people, may be of landlord origin, but may escape the landlord class category, and are permitted to retain double the average per capita holding of the area. Further exemption is made of elderly persons living alone, or orphans or invalids who have no alternative means of support.

This careful discrimination is part and parcel of the general principle of reasonableness and humanity which runs through present Chinese life, as indeed, to a considerable extent, it has always done.

3. The third step is confiscation and redistribution of the landlords' holdings. This is a less lengthy process than might be supposed, and generally needs no preliminary surveys or measurements. The local people, fully familiar with land ownership, already know the details.

General meetings are held, at which rich peasants and middle peasants are invited voluntarily to declare the extent of their holdings. Decisions on redistribution are taken. Three options for reconsideration are allowed. After that the decision is final. Only where subsistence is in question is compensation given. The medium, small, and law-abiding landlord is permitted to select for his own land that area which he, together with others, will receive at the redistribution.

4. The fourth and final step is the surrender of old title deeds and evidence of debt. These are burned in public, and new title deeds legalize the new holdings.

When the whole process has been completed in the base village, the news spreads and representatives are invited to come and witness its success. The trained personnel, with the exception of a small number for consolidation, then move on to other areas. A land reform commission in one place usually produces workers to deal with three other centers. Local government, Army and communications personnel all contribute help, as, for example, by laying telephone wires from the village to the county center.

Take, as an example, the concrete case of the procedure followed by Lao Duane in the Shuanghuaishu administrative area which embraced twelve villages.

One of the first tasks had been to purge and reorganize the local Peasants' Association. Ko Lin, the experienced head of the land reform team, had talked with Wang Yu, Chairman of the Association. His suspicions were aroused. Wang was a Peking shoemaker, not a peasant. The peasants themselves seemed afraid of assuming office, while Wang had packed the offices of the Association with men like himself. It turned out that Wang had been receiving gifts from landlord Kuan Chang-sheng; and when the work team arrived, he tried to make out that Kuan was really a middle peasant whose land must not be touched. The work team's first task was to mobilize the peasants to demand new elections and take office themselves. No easy task, but with patience achieved.

Of the twelve men and three women then elected, nine were poor peasants, four hired laborers, and two middle peasants: "All honest people."

To meet the peasants' fear of the feudal oppressors the team explained that the government was behind the Peasants' Association and that the landlords had lost all political power.

An Accusation Meeting was then called. A thousand villagers assembled. Two notorious landlords were arraigned. The people shouted: "Down with feudalism! Down with the despots!" The chairman said: "The time has come. Speak out all your grievances. You have nothing to fear. The Government, the Army, and the Militia all belong to us working people now."

Kuan was the target. He had been one of twenty-five men hired to guard the ancestral graveyard of a Manchu prince, and when the prince became bankrupt they had divided his land among themselves—five *mou* each. The Japanese came. Kuan turned traitor, went over to the enemy, and seized the land of the other twenty-four. He became village head, extracting taxes and selling young men as recruits for the puppet army.

Now Kuan was brought to justice.

"You black-hearted dog," shouted one old woman. "You grabbed our five *mou* of land, didn't you? And when my husband fell down from starvation, you told the Japanese he had an infectious disease and they burned him alive. True or not?"

"You took our land just before harvest," said another woman, "and kept our crop as well. You threw my son in jail and then offered him to the Japanese devils for their army. Where is my son now? Give him back to me. . . ."

When asked if the facts were true as stated, Kuan's voice was feeble; only the front row could hear. The Militia had to protect him from the people's rage.

On the basis of the evidence compiled at this meeting, the people's court sentenced Kuan Chang-sheng to four years' imprisonment.

Conditions were now ready to start the land distribution. First, every family had had its status determined, after the most careful classification. Then came the distribution of the "victory fruits." The average per capita land holding was two *mou* of dry land, and 1.5 *mou* of irrigated land. The landless peasants had first choice of vacant plots, while the cultivator of the land had prior claim to his own fields. Families which had fought in or aided the revolution had preferential treatment. Equal shares were distributed to the landlords' families, so that they could support themselves. The remaining land was distributed to the non-agricultural residents if they were willing to become farmers and had the necessary manpower.

Land liable to be requisitioned for industrial purposes was given rent free in the meantime to any who would till it: "And if the State should take the land back," says another peasant, "it means that a factory will go up and we can become workers if we want to."

Thus administered, the land reform gathered way. Success led to further success. It became all-pervasive. After 2,000 years of struggle, the peasant has won his right to live. By its redistribution law, the Communist Party has achieved the most drastic social revolution ever experienced in China and achieved a most profoundly moral act of justice.

In the first year after the promulgation of the Land Reform Law, 300,000 additional cadres, or teams of land reform workers, were trained. During 1951 land reform reached 130,000,000 rural people, or if we include the numbers for the old liberated areas, 320,000,000 people, *i.e.,* 80 percent of all those who live in the Chinese countryside.

The joy of China's farming community is profound and unbounded. So too is the joy of the small manufacturer and shopkeeper; for trade booms, owing to the new spending power of the farmers. Backwardness, poverty, and war recede as feudalism and imperialism, the breeding ground of all three, likewise recede.

LIBERATED WOMANHOOD

If the land reform completed the revolution for the farmer of China, it no less completed the revolution for his wife and daughters, who now share equally with husband and father in land proprietorship. I would even venture to suggest that the revolution in the case of women and girls is the greater of the two. Greater because more far-reaching.

Liberation of womanhood introduced a wholly new atmosphere into the home, that earliest and potentially happiest breeding ground and training ground of human relationships and fellowship.

Happiness in the home reacts upon life in all its activities; upon health, education, production. With real equality within its own borders and real harmony among its members the home becomes the most fruitful association in national life, realizing the truth of the old Chinese proverb: "When husband and wife go one way, sand and earth will turn into gold."

The division of the land, which has secured an equal share for each woman and girl as well as for each man and boy, has spelled economic freedom for womanhood. And, let it be noted, it is an economic freedom enjoyed nowhere yet in the Western world.

No longer is a woman of the agricultural class dependent economically upon her husband. She has her own land and her children have theirs. She ceases to be property. She owns property. She is independent. At one bound, she leaps out of a degradation unknown here, happily, for long centuries, if ever, and into a freedom as yet unattained even here.

Under feudalism the position of women was shockingly bad. At the outset the girl child was not wanted, save as a semi-slave for household work, or as a plaything and for purposes of breeding. Otherwise a girl in China was a liability. In maturity she could only be married off if possessed of an adequate dowry to attract a bridegroom.

In the China I knew in 1932 it was no uncommon thing for parents to leave a baby girl on a rubbish heap outside the city to die or to be eaten by dogs and birds. I visited in the Huai River Valley at that time the home of two elderly Protestant American ladies who mothered a large group of lovely, healthy children.

Many of them had been rescued as babes from a rubbish-heap death. The majority of parents, doubtless, loved their daughters. Still, boy babies were welcome; girls were not. Always at an economic disadvantage, they were only useful as semi-slaves or salable assets. In times of famine sale of a daughter was often the only escape from starvation for a whole family.

Again, girls under feudalism had no freedom to marry whom they would. Neither, for that matter, had boys. Many girls were married to total strangers, sometimes to senile or infirm old men. Marriages were arranged by the parents. Mao Tse-tung himself was married at fourteen to a girl of twenty, whom he never liked. It was "arranged" for him.

Rich landlords could afford many wives. Indeed, wives became an economic asset to the rich. They worked without pay; the only expense was for food and clothes. In Fuyan district, Anwei Province, there was a landlord who, right up to the time of the land reform, had seventy wives. He justified it on the score of economy: "It is more economical to keep many wives than to employ workers; wives work hard without pay." In many cases wives were insulted, exploited, maltreated, or regarded as mere toys to be broken like a child's doll when no longer desired.

In old China, and in Kuomintang China, a widower might marry, a widow never. Woe betide the widow who did. A widow in Huai Yang district of Honan Province, whose husband had been dead for eight years, taking advantage of the new marriage law, married by free choice Yang Tien-chen, the headman of the village. Her uncle, Chen Pri-lien, a local despot not yet dislodged, heard of it and denounced her. She had brought shame on the family. He, her brother, and her brother-in-law descended upon her. "There is only one solution," they said, "commit suicide." She refused. They beat her to death.

Women, in general were never on an equal footing with men. They lived a slave-like existence, the chattel, the toy, or the drudge of their husbands and often, and perhaps worse still, of their mothers-in-law.

The Communist Government planned a radical change. Women had earned their freedom in the struggle against the Japanese, the Kuomintang, the feudal landlords. They had earned reward. They received full freedom, crowned by economic freedom. By the promulgation of the new Marriage Law in 1950 women are guaranteed the right by law to freedom of marriage.

The change had earlier origins. The "May 4th Movement" in 1919 ushered in the new democratic period in China's Revolution. During the ensuing years Chinese women joined ranks with the forward-looking masses in the struggle against imperialism, feudalism, bureaucratic capitalism, and the reactionary rule of the Kuomintang. Women participated actively in the whole series of revolutionary movements: the May 4th Movement in 1919, the May 30th Movement in 1935, the northern expedition against the warlords in 1924, the Agrarian Reform, the Resistance War against the Japanese in 1937-45, and the People's Liberation War.*

* For these and other significant events, see the historical section, "Party and Army."—*Ed.*

Working women and revolutionary intellectuals made heroic sacrifices and achieved increasing solidarity. Women were indispensable in defeating the enemy. They are indispensable in constructing the New China. They had earned their freedom, and they won it. Now they are repaying a hundredfold the gift they have received.

An excellent and heroic example of what women can do and have done is Chun-ching. We met her in Hankow on International Children's Day in 1952, when we spoke at a mighty rally of young pioneers, the children being entertained by a children's own performance in a large hall.

Let me quote from my wife's diary:

"Across the central gangway from where I sat were one or two women: Labor Heroines, wearing their medals, and a young soldier boy—or so I thought, until I was told her story.

"Kuo Chun-ching's parents were very poor. Her father was tortured to death by the Japanese. Her mother in despair tried to sell her as a slave to a rich landlord. Kuo Chun-ching escaped, cut off her hair, dressed up as a boy and fled to the Resistance Army.

"She joined as a boy in 1945 and fought with the Army for five years until 1950, during which time she had gained one of the highest awards that China offers for bravery.

"Not until 1950 was it discovered that she was a girl, nineteen years old.

"Kuo Chun-ching became one of China's heroines, an example of the heroic bravery of tens of thousands of ordinary women, who fought for years against the Japanese and against the Kuomintang. We spent most of the day with her. She was modest and quiet and retiring, but it was wonderful to see the honor in which the children held her and how proud the men and women with us were even to meet her and with what deference they regarded her."

The achievement, however, of women's liberation has been far from easy. There have been many lessons to learn. Women like men have made mistakes. The documents of the Women's Movement in China lie before me, and I can trace the Wise Counsel by following which women have become the powerful and constructive force they are today.

The Wise Counsel began in 1948 in the liberated areas, where the land reform had been completed. A fundamental change had taken place in class relations in the villages, for all alike, young and old, men and women, had received a portion of land. Many women were elected as district and village representatives. The political and social consciousness of women had been raised, together with their economic, social, and domestic status. The door had been prized open for complete emancipation of Chinese women.

In some areas defects had appeared which if not checked might become dangerous. As, for example, the use of slogans in place of mastering technique and doing things. To shout on every occasion "Freedom of marriage," "Economic independence," was useless unless while the men were fighting the women backed them up by practical contributions to the work that must be done if life was to be carried on and the war of liberation won. The Wise Counsel urged that economic work was the greatest and most appropriate contribution women could make to the revolutionary war at that period.

Furthermore, women working hard in production and earning money thereby were the more respected. In that way they strengthened the fight against feudal bondage, against those who maltreated the girl bride, against foot-binding and other ill practices.

Most important of all, they learned by experience and taught by experience that economic independence is the key for promoting the political and social status of women, for raising their cultural level and winning complete emancipation.

Production has become the center of women's work. It is by the ladder of economic independence that women have climbed to social and political equality with men. They received their just reward when the New Land Distribution Law clinched the matter and made women and children equal recipients of China's "good earth."

The results became apparent at once and now expand. Women enlisted with enthusiasm side by side with men in the great construction projects. Over 300,000 women took part in the Chun-kiang and Huai River schemes.

Let me again quote from my wife's diary:

"In Pengpu [on the Huai River] we met another Labor Heroine. Her story, too, told of the difference between the old life for women and children and all the peasants, and the new life into which they are throwing themselves with such ardor and enthusiasm.

"At the exhibition of the Huai River project hung a large oil painting of a group of women with one girl leading them. Her name was Gan Tsai-hua.

"Gan Tsai-hua belonged to a peasant family, living in a village outside Pengpu. Life was terribly hard, with many floods and constant famine. Many lost their lives in the floods—and in the famines that followed whole families were wiped out. Added to all that was the war. The life of the women was one of incessant labor, haunted by incessant threat of death.

"Just before the Liberation Armies came, Gan's village had the Kuomintang troops billeted in their homes for five months. Nothing was safe. No one was safe. The soldiers took everything—food, animals, even

It was by the ladder of economic independance that women climbed to social and political equality with men.

clothes. The people had nothing to eat, nothing to work with, nothing to wear. As Gan put it graphically: 'Not even a matchstick was left. People could not live.'

"Then the Kuomintang were driven away and the People's Liberation Army came. The people received them with ecstatic joy, and they, in turn, helped the people with everything. They brought them food. They gave them clothing. There was only one very old mule left in the whole village, but the Army men helped to do what the draught animals had done.

"Later came land reform and each woman and each girl had her own share of land.

"In 1950 there was a bad flood and Chairman Mao Tse-tung said the Huai River must be harnessed. After three months' planning, the work began. Peasants and farmers were eager to share in the work. All their lives they had lived in fear of the river.

"Gan Tsai-hua organized a team of women in her village. There were forty-seven in her team, the youngest seventeen, the oldest forty. She led them to the work and organized them there. In the winter, when the temperature was 15 degrees below zero, the ice had to be broken and removed. Who would do this job?

"Gan Tsai-hua took her shoes off and, jumping into the bitter cold water, started to break up the ice. Calling to the other women of her team to follow her, united they did the job. 'Chairman Mao and our Government do so much for us, the people: we, the people, are eager to do all we can in return,' explained Gan Tsai-hua, repeating it many times."

The Common Program, which is now authoritative for China, and acts as a Constitution, clinching the matter, provides for full emancipation of women. Article 6 states: "The People's Republic of China shall abolish the feudal system which holds women in bondage. Women shall enjoy equal rights with men in political, economic, cultural, educational and social life. Freedom of marriage for men and women shall be put into effect."

Long operating in the liberated areas, these liberties for women have now become the law of all China. This elevation of women to take part in governmental work on an equal footing with men is an event unprecedented in the 5,000 years of China's history.

The whole round of social effects is outstanding. Take the new marriage laws. Not only have women complete freedom to marry whom they will, not only can marriage no longer be arranged for them, but they are free as widows to remarry when and to whom they will.

I can never forget the story of one woman told to us in a land-divided village. She had been left a widow at an early age. Longing for a husband, longing for children, she was denied both. She must remain from early girlhood to old age a lonely widow. Then came the New Marriage Law.

Widows could marry if they wished to do so. She married a widower with two children and had one of her own. It was a proud and happy home for both. Recipients of land, they had been able to build a new house with more accommodation and greater amenities, and there they proudly entertained us.

Chen Hsiao-ni, to quote another case from a village in Shansi Province, was engaged to a man while still a child. The marriage was unhappy, and she dreamed of running away to end her suffering. The New Marriage Law was announced. She claimed a divorce. Married to a man of her own choice, she now lives happily with her husband, working together with him to improve their crops, and helping ten other women to improve the technique of their own field work.

Women, again, are working in every branch of the national economy. By December, 1952, they numbered 990,000, a 74 percent increase over 1950. Women in 1951 constituted 8.6 percent of China's 86,500 model workers.

The methods of Ho Chien-hsiu, woman spinner in the State Cotton Mill at Tsingtao, reduced the rate of cotton wastage 86.5 percent below the national average. Setting a standard for other mills, she has effected enormous savings.

Women in industry receive equal pay with men for equal work, and the wage rates in 1952 increased from 60 to 120 percent above 1949. Also and increasingly they are provided with nursery schools and crèches, without which the home would suffer.

In the country 40 million women have joined the Peasants' Associations, giving invaluable help in land reform, in which 700 million *mou* of good land has been distributed among more than 300 million men and women. Millions upon millions of peasant women work hard to create record harvests. In most villages more than 60 percent of the women take part in agricultural labor, while between 40 and 60 percent of the total number of women in agriculture have joined mutual-aid teams and agricultural producers' co-operatives.

The political fruits also followed speedily. A considerable number of women were elected district and village representatives and mounted to even higher rank. Beginning with a modest share in mutual aid groups, women were elected at length to some of the highest offices of State. Though the Chinese People's Republic was only born in October, 1949, there were already sixty-nine women delegates, or more than 10 percent of the total, at the First Plenary Session of the Chinese People's Consultative Council, which exercised the power of an All-China People's Congress. In 1952 it was 15 percent; in Peking 18 percent of the People's representatives. In local street community centers in Peking the proportion of women has increased to 48 percent.

Women begin to occupy important positions in the People's Government at all levels, magnificently led by Madame Sun Yat-sen, widow of the founder of the Chinese Republic. Resisting all temptations to join with her sisters—one the wife of Chiang Kai-shek, another the wife of Doctor Kung, the corrupt Minister of Finance—or her brother, T. V. Soong, Chiang Kai-shek's Foreign Minister, Ching-ling, as she is called in China, remained steadfast in the progressive cause, determined to carry out her husband's principles, co-operation with the Communist Party and friendship with the Soviet Union. She saved the lives of hundreds of China's progressives and risked her own in doing so.

Today Madame Sun Yat-sen is Vice-Chairman of the People's Republic of China.

Madame Li Teh-chuan is Minister of Health.

Madame Chou En-lai is Chairman of the Democratic Women's Federation.

Not only in the industrial but also in the cultural field women press on. The mass of Chinese women are illiterate, a defect being conquered with speed and enthusiasm.

Millions of women are attending schools for adults, literacy and evening classes. Even in 1951 half of the 42 million peasants of both sexes attending winter schools were women.

Women have their own organizations for their own peculiar problems: some 40,000 cadres were developing work among women all over the country in 1952.

Never before in all history has the world witnessed such an upsurge on such a scale as this.

I would only add that the warm and spontaneous affection of Gan Tsai-hua for my wife was one of the most moving things I saw in China. She held her hand all the afternoon and hardly loosed it when we dined at night. But indeed, this warmth of Chinese women to peace-loving women of other lands was well-nigh universal. If their wills are steel and their courage dauntless, their hearts are as warmly responsive as a child's. By intuition they seem instantaneously to know who loves them, and they give all their love in return. This affection and this devotion to duty, and their gratitude for help and sympathy finding outlets everywhere, are indeed a symbol of the harvest that is reaped from the liberation of China's womanhood.

2 China's Natural Enemies Defeated

FLOOD MENACE ENDED

CHINA'S farmers and China's farmers' wives are freed from feudal foes. They are masters of the land they till. But other enemies which menace them are to be fought with equal resolution: flood, drought, famine. The rivers of China, untamed, are a peril to all. Liberated China fights to tame them, and fights to win.

Flooded rivers are no new problem in China. They are an age-long menace. But never has China tackled water control or water conservation with the same science, the same vigor and the same measure of success or with future prospects more bright, than now in 1952, less than three years after Liberation.

The earthwork excavated—largely by manual labor, through lack of adequate modern machinery—in three years is equal to the earthwork excavated for ten Panama Canals or twenty-three Suez Canals. In 1952 the investment on water conservation projects was fifty-two times the highest sum spent by the Kuomintang regime in any one year. The area of land liable to be stricken has been greatly reduced. In 1949 the area affected was 8 million hectares (1 hectare = 2.5 acres) reduced in 1950 to 4,600,000 hectares, in 1951 to 1,400,000, and in 1952 to still less.

The Yangtze, the Yellow River, the Huai River, the Yi River, the Pearl River, the Tungting Lake, and many more projects constantly appear on the blueprints of China's Water Conservation Program. It is hard to know where to begin. Best, perhaps, begin with a geographical picture of the land itself, which gives birth and form to China's mighty waterways.

The landscape of China comprises high plateaus in the northwest, with slopes or declinations to the southeast, where lowlands or hilly terrain, interspersed with basins, have been formed. That is why most of the rivers rise in the northwest, flow through loess plateaus or mountain gorges, and then in their southeasterly flow shape the alluvial plains of the coast.

The two best-known rivers, the Yangtze and the Yellow River, drain the central and southern lands. Between them lies the highly important Huai River with its fan-shaped drainage area and its direct connections with its two great neighbors.

The Yangtze and the Yellow River, great in length, are the main arterial waterways of China. At Hankow, 600 miles inland from the sea, the Yangtze measures a mile from shore to shore; sea-going ships can harbor in its docks.

The Yangtze carries half the domestic trade of China. Busy and famous ports line is banks—Shanghai, Nanking, Hankow, Shasi, Ichang, Chungking.

The Yangtze has over 25,000 miles of navigable water in the main river and its tributaries.

On the whole, the Yangtze is a good and safe river, but it has its danger spots and danger periods. The 186-mile-long middle section is a bottle-neck and a menace. The river narrows at a point where it has received the waters, swift and turbulent in July, from many tributaries. The river in spate at Shasi, situated in the bottle-neck reaches 2,100,000 cubic feet per second; the main channel has a capacity of only 1,600,000 cubic feet. The river rises 30 feet and more above the surrounding land. The old dykes were weak. Breaks and disasters were frequent.

No previous Chinese government ever aided local efforts at flood control here or elsewhere. The Manchus, indeed, collected money for the purpose, and with it cast a series of iron bulls to control the waters by "magic"; they pocketed the major part of the taxes.

Not that China was entirely powerless from a scientific point of view. Flood and drought in China were not entirely due to lack of knowledge. China for 1,000 years has possessed capable hydraulic engineers. In Shensi, Ningsia, Shansi, and Szechuan Provinces irrigation channels still exist which were dug by peasants in the Chin and Han Dynasties. When I journeyed in 1932 to the west and north with Major Todd, who was then executing wide schemes of irrigation and river control on the Yellow and King Rivers, he pointed out the commemoration stones recording the completion of various irrigation schemes for many centuries back.

Water-control schemes were never wanting in China. But as often as not they were left as blueprints, or graft prevented their completion; at best they were but partial. Never was there a program with a range like that of New China's water conservation program. But what amazes me most of all as an ex-engineer, knowing what the Kuomintang did or failed to do, is the speed with which Liberated China is now mastering her own wide range of major water problems. And in no instance was this more marked than in the flood control project of the Middle Yangtze in 1952.

June 20, 1952, marked the completion of a major control project which removes the peril of the middle section, where the Yangtze is called the Chin River.

The chief feature of the project is a huge detention basin of 900 square kilometers on the south side of the river, with a capacity of over seven billion cubic meters of water. This relieves the narrow, winding section of the Yangtze of the flood excess.

The flow is controlled by three huge dams. That for the intake to the detention basin, over 1,000 yards long with 54 sluice gates, is located at Taipington. This is the largest sluice in China. Another, 369 yards long, with 32 sluice gates, adjacent to the south end of the basin, conducts a further section of the Yangtze flood flowing through the Hutu River into the Tungting Lake, which also serves as a detention basin.

The third dam, at Wuliangan, conducts the water back into the Yangtze under safe conditions when the flood subsides.

Dyke walls, planted with shelter belts of trees, enclose the detention basin.

Drainage channels quickly empty the basin of flood water and permit the planting of winter crops in the enriched soil in the low-water season.

It was breath-taking to stand beside the new construction work at Chinkiang on the middle Yangtze River in mid-June of 1952 and gaze along that immense battery of semicircular steel shields, each high as a cottage and long as a cricket pitch—massive shields, coupled by powerful girders to the axis on which they revolve admitting or excluding the water at will as need demands—fifty-four of them, stretching far away into the distance, and connected by a vast paved roadway to the Yangtze, ready to receive the flood waters as they rise and conduct them to the detention basin, there to rest until the floods recede. Afterward, the flood waters are permitted to flow slowly and safely back through other mighty gates to the lower reaches of the river, into the Tungting Lake.

That vast project of water gates and dykes, hundreds of miles long, for the construction of which most contractors would demand years, took, from first to last, less than three months to complete. And in one of those months, work proceeded in torrents of rain.

We were in Hangchow, taking a three days' rest, midway through our seven weeks' hard travel and study, when an invitation to visit this great construction came. Returning from a quiet cruise in a leisurely rowboat to the Lily Pond Island on the Hangchow Lake, we were enjoying from our windows the same peaceful beauty of town and water which had thrilled Marco Polo 600 years earlier—"Heaven above and Hangchow below," is China's picturesque description of this charming town—when we received an urgent telephone message from Peking:

"Would you care to see the last days of construction and the opening day ceremony of the Chinkiang Project on the middle Yangtze? If so, please proceed at once to Shanghai, where a special plane from Peking will meet you and take you to Hankow, and thence by river steamer to the construction itself."

Of course we seized the opportunity, met the plane at Shanghai and arrived at Shasi just before completion of the work and in time to see the final stage in full swing.

Who that has seen such work and such methods can ever forget the sight! Three hundred thousand men at work! Strenuous work. Skilled and understanding work. Not a man without his clearly defined and eagerly pursued job. Standing on top of the dykes or on the great steel and concrete construction itself one looked across the leveling plain, watched mountains of earth melt away, or stone-faced pavements nearly a yard thick advance as by magic to one's feet. Most dramatic of all was the sigh of the stalwart brown bodies of the Red Army men, clad only in dark blue, white-striped shorts, winding, like the evolutions of a giant ballet, in and out of other workers, following some pattern of their own.

Two million peasants in all have worked on this outstanding project. No hardships frightened the workers, no problems daunted the engineers. Many were the difficulties surmounted.

For example, the ground planned for the base of the new dyke at the furthermost point of the detention area proved to be feet deep in mud.

This must be cleared away to receive the broad footing of the dyke walls; how to clear it was the problem.

No modern pumping machine had arrived or could arrive. So men did it, 30,000 of them, and often quite literally with their own hands.

A battery of fifty two massive shields stretching nearly three quarters of a mile---- ready to receive the flood-water.

Unable to walk to and fro through the deep mire, men passed the mud from hand to hand, using in addition any such vessels—and they were very few—as they could procure. Red Army men by the thousands joined in. High officers took part, filling their mackintosh coats with mud and passing them also along the line.

Incredible feats were achieved. And the project was done in time. Done before the peak floods came with threats to eight million souls.

No wonder excitement ran high on this the opening day of China's new water project. Mao Tse-tung and his gallant band had said as they studied the speedily drawn up maps and plans: "The work must be done before the summer floods arrive." And done it was. For the whole countryside was behind Mao Tse-tung. Each farmer as he worked on dyke or sluices knew that his wife, his children, and his property were at stake. He knew that the national food supply was at stake. And others knew it too. So the whole of China's engineering shops, steel mills, and cement factories and the mechanics who worked in them, as well as the farmers who directly benefited, were behind Mao Tse-tung. It was a nationwide job and a nationwide achievement.

We arrived in time to visit the works on the eve of completion. Excitement ran mountains high. As our steamer neared the landing stage at Shasi, the banks were lined with men, women, and children to greet us. Vast crowds had assembled and pioneers presented flowers which well nigh smothered us. Bands played and silken banners flew. And then the mile-long drive in jeeps through the cheering crowds, children flinging flowers onto our laps and flights of doves into the air.

There was something deeply moving in their pride and joy that foreigners, *British* foreigners, should see and share in the completion of one of China's most mighty, most peaceful, most humane, and most constructive tasks in all her long, checkered history.

Here too, for the first time, was a scheme in which none suffered, as formerly some were sure to suffer when dykes aided one area at the cost of others. None suffered from the middle Yangtze project. Farmers in the newly flooded 900 square kilometers of catchment water had safe refuge homes for themselves, their families, their goods, and their cattle, out of reach of the highest floods. Safety areas where they could stay during the few weeks ere the flood waters were drawn off, thence to return to prepare the enriched land for the spring crops, rice or wheat, of which one or two harvests could be reaped before the July rains again sent them to the safety zone. None suffered. All shared the rich benefits of the new middle Yangtze water project.

And yet this middle Yangtze project, despite its vast significance, was only a single aspect of a wider, more comprehensive scheme of Yangtze

River control; one act of a drama which will stretch out for years until the entire plan of Yangtze conservation, with its enlarged transport facilities, its vast irrigation areas and incredible electric power supplies, is completed. It is of incalculable value to have seen it. But for a complete and rounded whole, now approaching completion, we must turn next to the Huai River Project.

TAMED WATERS

It was of incalculable value, as we said, to have seen the 1952 Yangtze Water Project. But that, as we also observed, is but a torso of a vaster scheme projected in the future. For the blueprint of a comprehensive and now largely completed scheme we must turn to the Huai River Project, the most interesting of all the schemes scheduled on China's water conservation program.

The Huai is one of China's bigger rivers, yielding in size only to its great neighbors, the Yellow River in the north and the Yangtze in the south. Rising in the Tung Po Mountain, the Huai descends steeply down from the highlands and then runs on through the plains of the important provinces of Honan, Anhwei, and Kiangsu.

Ten large tributaries and many smaller ones feed it. The Huai itself is normally calm, deep, and navigable, and has been called "The Young Maiden." But some of its tributaries are steep and turbulent, their inflow in the months of July and August causing floods and havoc, aggravated by four bottle necks along the course of the main stream.

The devastations caused by the flooding of the Huai River have been terrible. It was the great flood of 1931 which took me to China with a message of sympathy when in 1932 I traveled through the Huai Valley in the middle reaches and along the Grand Canal to the Yangtze. The sufferings had been indescribable; some 147 million *mou* of land had been submerged and the lives of 52 million people shattered. Many were the deaths through drowning or subsequent starvation. There was another devastating disaster in 1950.

Huai River disasters are a story as old as they are terrible. The Huai River alone has registered 973 floods between 246 B.C. and A.D. 1948, a flood every two years for seventy generations, with a major flood on an average every ten years and a vast catastrophe every eighty or 100 years.

Never, however, until now, during all those generations, has any radical scheme of control, all-embracing for the needs of an area which contains

50 million peasants and covers one-seventh of all China's cultivated land, been applied or contemplated.

These disasters are to cease. The Huai River is to be harnessed and turned to profitable tasks. By July, 1951, the first stage of a three-to-five-year plan had been completed. By the end of 1952 the peasants of the Huai Valley already enjoyed a security never known before.

The main Huai River is 683 miles long, having more than 200 tributaries, large and small. It covers an area of 220,000 square kilometers containing 171,500,000 *mou* of land and numbers upward of 50,000,000 in population, rather more than that of Britain. The Huai Valley is indeed a densely populated rural area.

Before the Sung Dynasty, the Huai River had been peaceful with a sufficiency of pools and ponds to irrigate the land. The break-through of the Yellow River in 1194 brought disaster which subsequent dynasties, Sung, Yuan, Ming, or Manchu Ching, did little to mitigate. Rather in later years, due to endless annexation of land, reckless cutting down of trees for timber, and the transformation of ponds into farmland by landlords and rich farmers, the people were robbed of the harnessed waters and, most disastrous of all, robbed of the flood-storage capacity for the safety of the Huai River itself. This resulted in uneven distribution of rainfall and in the yearly silting up of river beds with mud and sand.

Despotic emperors, to maintain the water supply for the Grand Canal, which runs north to south across the east-west lower reaches of the Huai River, and to facilitate the transportation of their own rice supplies, had built dykes along the western bank of the canal to check the current. This raised the water level in the Huai River. The internal waters, dammed up, turned into lakes. Floods then brought disasters, one of which I observed in 1932, when a Grand Canal dyke had been breached.

The crowning disaster came in 1938, when, for military reasons, and without fully calculating or regarding the consequences, Chiang Kai-shek deliberately broke the southern dyke of the Yellow River which had in 1855 turned once more to its northern sea exits with nearly a century of readjustment. Fourteen million *mou* of farmland were submerged. More than half a million people died and another half million were forced to flee. The disastrous diversion continued during the subsequent nine years. The entire lower course of the Huai River was ruined.

Throughout China's history no effort has ever been made to harness the entire Huai River. Because of that, the burden was merely shifted from one shoulder to another. Partial harnessing in one direction led to disaster in another. The projects which had been imposed on the people, such, for example, as the Hungtse Dyke project, only added to the menace, through their damage to other areas. The Kuomintang's large talk of harnessing the Huai River had led to nothing.

In 1950, when the Huai River was suffering the most recent flood of its history, the people were informed of Chairman Mao's decision: "The Huai River must be harnessed." Allocating grain, salt, coal, winter clothing, and medicine for temporary relief, the government laid its plans for radical mastery of the river. The people likewise, encouraged by this positive assistance, began to organize themselves. They prepared the tools necessary to wage determined struggle against the floods which had harassed them and their land for over 1,000 years. The whole valley rejoiced and braced itself for its vast tasks.

This Huai River project is the most important and interesting of all the water-control schemes scheduled in China's water conservation program. Indeed, it is the most important all-round water project ever undertaken in China's long history, and that for the following reasons:

1. It masters, in an entirely new and radical way, an age-long peril.
2. It forms a self-contained and complete scheme for an area rich in agricultural possibilities, securing safety and prosperity for a population of more than 50 million people.
3. It assures the solution of China's food problem.
4. It meets within a single scheme the fourfold need of—
   (a) Flood protection.
   (b) Provision of electric power.
   (c) Irrigation.
   (d) Deepening and lengthening of a whole network of navigable channels.
5. It tackles the river problem from source to sea, providing for—
   (a) Protection from the incursion of the Yellow River.
   (b) Reservoirs in the deep gorges at the source of ten and more tributaries.
   (c) Planting of trees to stay the floods on the steep mountainsides.
   (d) Deepening the channels.
   (e) Systematic provision of catchment lakes and dykes.
   (f) Cutting a new and navigable channel direct to the Yellow Sea.
6. It enlists the sympathy and assures the co-operation of the community of farmers and others throughout the whole vast area which its fan-shaped network embraces.

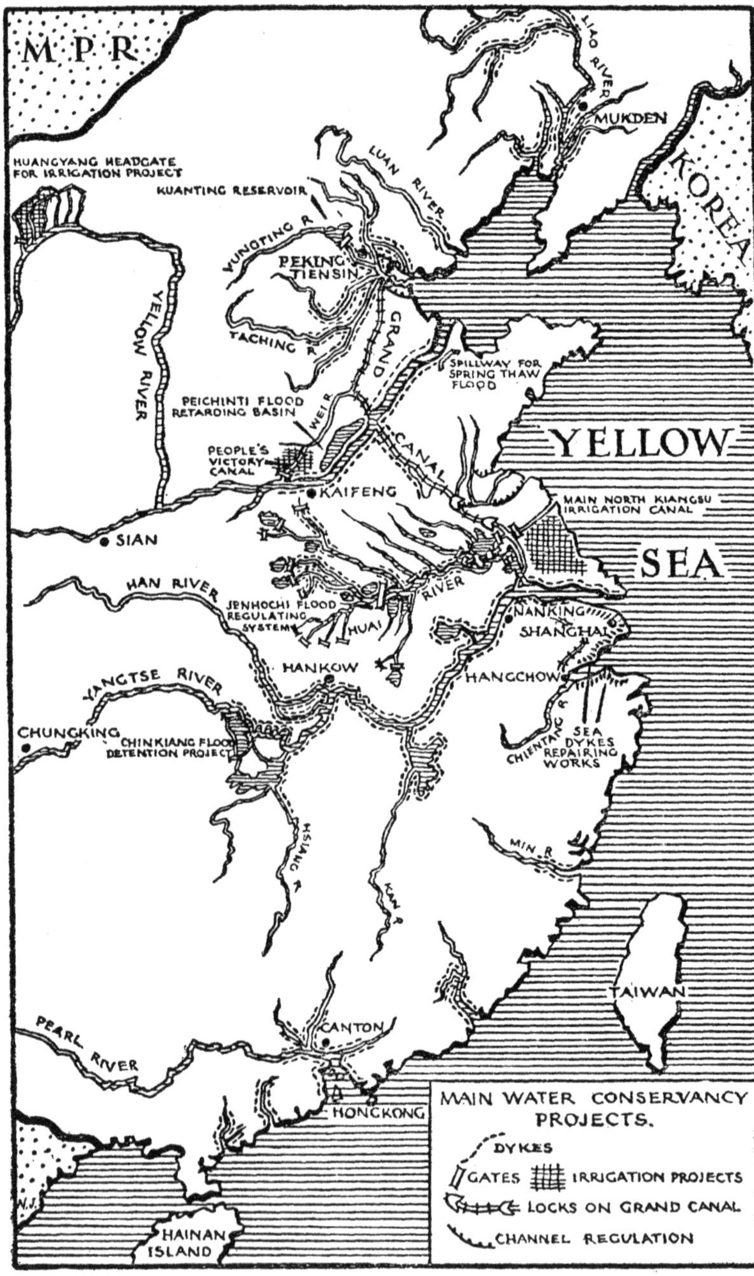
M.P.R.
HUANGYANG HEADGATE FOR IRRIGATION PROJECT
KUANTING RESERVOIR
LUAN RIVER
LIAO RIVER
MUKDEN
KOREA
YUNGTING R.
PEKING
TIENSIN
TACHING R.
GRAND
CANAL
YELLOW RIVER
SPILLWAY FOR SPRING THAW FLOOD
PEICHINTI FLOOD RETARDING BASIN
WEI R.
PEOPLE'S VICTORY CANAL
KAIFENG
YELLOW
SEA
MAIN NORTH KIANGSU IRRIGATION CANAL
SIAN
HAN RIVER
RIVER
JENHOCHI FLOOD REGULATING SYSTEM
HUAI
NANKING
SHANGHAI
HANKOW
HANGCHOW
YANGTSE RIVER
CHUNGKING
CHINKIANG FLOOD DETENTION PROJECT
CHIENTANG R.
SEA DYKES REPAIRING WORKS
HSIANG R.
KAN R.
MIN R.
TAIWAN
CANTON
PEARL RIVER
HONGKONG
N.J.
HAINAN ISLAND
MAIN WATER CONSERVANCY PROJECTS.
DYKES
GATES
IRRIGATION PROJECTS
LOCKS ON GRAND CANAL
CHANNEL REGULATION

7. It originates from, and has the whole-hearted and powerful support of, the Liberation Government.

8. It has focused the eyes of all China upon a gigantic test scheme and won the eager support of engineers, steelworkers, machinemakers, cement operatives, and a host of other workers.

9. It enlists the skilled services of women as well as men. The engineer second in control of the whole scheme, and with sole control of its central area, is a woman.

Government administration got immediately to work; it mapped out a policy of "detaining and expelling flood water at the same time," with benefit to the three provinces, "transforming the threat into a benefit." A Huai River Harnessing Committee was to carry out this prior task.

The Committee decided to work out a plan: (1) to control flood, (2) to regulate the course of the river and its tributaries, (3) to open up more channels and lakes in order to detain sufficient water along the upper, middle, and lower reaches of the entire Huai River, to prevent overflow and to provide an ample and secure navigation system.

The Hungtse Lake, near the mouth of the river, was to be so controlled that it could not only regulate the main body of the Huai River, but also irrigate the 25 million *mou* of farm lands in North Kiangsu.

The final items on the schedule were soil conservation in the mountainous districts, with extensive digging of ditches, pools, and ponds in the plains, dredging the river and developing irrigation.

"Gorge-type" reservoirs in the highlands, catchment lakes in the lowlands, were the two main methods used for flood control.

The gorge-type reservoirs—there will be some thirteen of them when complete—built in valleys with small outlets through enclosed valley mouths, but with big space in their upper reaches, are not planned merely for water catchment to prevent floods, though that is their primary object. They will supply a controllable reserve for irrigation, waterpower, and navigation, serving an area of 40,000 square kilometers.

Soil will be conserved by large-scale planting of trees and introduction of terrace farming. The landscape will change.

The conservation of the head waters of the tributary rivers will be supplemented by seventeen lakes along the Huai River itself.

These, with the aid of their regulating works, gates, levees, and culverts, will control the floods at human will and speed the development of irrigation.

This latter point is important, because not only is the river capacity incapable of dealing with the excessive rainfall in July, August, and September, but the lack of captured, retained, and controlled water in the dry nine months of the year led to drought.

Hitherto the lakes were merely swamps, pestilential and useless for agriculture. Filling up before the peak of the flood came, they were useless for flood control.

Now they are drained and will cultivate at least one crop a year and be ready to catch and retain the flood waters at the peak periods.

At the heart of this chain of lakes and checks, and midway down the main Huai River, is the Jenhochi Water Regulating System, which was completed in 1951 and now controls eight lakes with a storage capacity of 5,800,000,000 cubic meters of water. Its sluice gates across the main river, similar to those I saw on the Yangtze, will be 300 meters wide with another series of sluices leading to the retaining lake, 179 meters wide.

The big steel sluice gates, 45 meters wide, were produced in 120 factories in Shanghai after forty days and nights of intensive work.

The whole of this huge unit, completed in less than 100 days, carried the Huai River safely through the flood season of 1951. The Hungtse Lake will be controlled by still larger sluice gates and will hold six billion cubic meters of water.

The Huai River itself will be protected by 915 kilometers of dykes and by dredging of its channels.

This tedious and laborious work of dredging, dyking, and other construction work on contributary rivers also proceeds on the main Huai River: 270,000 rural workers have toiled incessantly at this task through the bitter cold of a Chinese winter. It was here that Gan Tsai-hua, in her enthusiastic determination that winter weather should not hinder the completion of the project to secure summer safety for the people, broke the ice to continue the digging. After eighty days of intensive labor, the diggers had completed a vast range of earthworks which now protects 2,500,000 *mou* of farm lands.

The smooth flow of the Chungtung River demanded the construction of a new channel, 24 kilometers long, now through quicksands and now through low hills involving cuttings 70 to 80 feet deep.

As the whole Huai River scheme is comprehensive, providing for irrigation as well as protection from flood, it involved the provision of a main irrigation canal in north Kiangsu, 170 kilometers in length, prepared by 800,000 rural workers continuing their operation through the winter of 1950 and the spring of 1951. As a result, 5,800,000 *mou* of miscellaneous crops, 5 million *mou* of cotton fields, and 15 million *mou* of rice fields will be irrigated by ditches, ponds, and pools, bringing the total up to 20 million *mou*. China's food problems are reaching solution. No longer supplicating grain from America, China donates grain to India.

Navigation along four great channels—the main river and its three large tributaries, totaling more than 2,000 kilometers—is now available for steamships of 300 tons. Steamships below 50 tons can sail along tributaries right up to the hilly areas.

In places near the gorge-type reservoirs strong streams with potential water power will be used to generate electricity for power supply.

In a very real sense, the whole of this comprehensive Huai Valley Conservation construction is a people's work. In the first year two million eager workers constructed 200 million cubic meters of earthworks. Transport for one million tons of material was needed, and often over long distances. Junk owners were eager to contribute their craft and their labor.

We spent an afternoon on one lovely junk in the main Huai River, enjoying the smooth glide of these graceful craft with their light golden timbers shining with tung-oil polish. The owner told us that his junk, one of 9,000, had worked night and day during the times of pressure taking loads of material far up to the face of the work.

Every stroke of work was made for the security and prosperity of all and each. And all knew it. Junk owners were no longer haunted by fear of unemployment; waterways were accessible far into the interior and farmers in the new prosperity had always goods to send and goods to seek.

Within five years, of which more than two and a half have already gone, this vast scheme will be completed. The toughest part is already well up to schedule time. The remainder is mainly drudgery. But the two million workers dread drudgery as little as technicians dread problems.

And the problems have been by no means few.

The key points for control of the tributary waters from the upper reaches, to take a significant instance of difficulty, is Chenyanghuan. There the river in spate in 1950 registered more cubic meters per second than the capacity of the channel below Chenyanghuan could take. That spelled disaster.

Above Chenyanghuan are eight lakes and swamps, lying lower than the river and with large capacity.

The solution was obvious: its execution difficult, costly, and arduous. Sever the lakes from the main river. Strengthen the existing dykes. Throw a dam at the upper end to admit the heavy flood water when use of a catchment basin was needed.

The lie of the land at Jenhochi lent itself to this comprehensive regulating scheme, making it possible, by separating the main river from the adjoining lakes, to give adequate storage in order to reduce the maximum discharge at Chenyanghuan to a safe limit.

That task has already been completed and the summer flooding has been conquered. Difficulties of execution arose. The masses of steel and concrete used in the construction of huge modern dams with their complicated sluices needed stout and durable foundations for their support. Bukhov, the Russian adviser, assured the Chinese engineers that by employing new methods it could be done with the available Chinese labor, Chinese technicians, and Chinese material.

To prove his contention, Bukhov suggested fundamentally new methods of construction for the foundation of the dam. No one in China had ever dreamed of foundations on soil without the aid of piles. But piles for the dam in question at Jenhochi would involve 12,000 30-foot poles, with three months to drive them in. Neither the piles nor the time were available. Work on the old method could not be completed to meet the 1951 floods.

Bukhov explained the modern Russian method. The huge Russian dams rest wholly on soil, with no support from piles, which in Russia are considered dangerous, aiding, among other objections, underground water percolation.

A new design, so contrived that water pressure of any water load would be directed to the center of the base, was prepared. The water then in every case fixed the dam down on its center; the more water, the more secure the whole dam became. Following this method, vast savings were effected in time and material. The result proved entirely successful.

Difficulties of treacherous soil were similarly conquered by the Russian method of excavating two meters deep and refilling the space with coarse sand. Difficulties of seepage were met by a series of impervious clay blankets in place of wooden piles or steel structures.

The whole construction has achieved signal success. Its smooth execution was due to the fact that it depended upon the people and the Government and not upon contractors. All were interested in achieving the goal.

All were conscientious. All knew what was at stake. All were interested because the interests of all were involved. And all were willing to learn. Young engineers, leaving their offices and drawing boards, went out into the field and, working with the skilled technicians and craftsmen, gained first-hand knowledge of the details of foundation excavation, of making reinforcements, of contraction and expansion of joints, of the pouring of concrete and the co-ordination of various processes.

Hence not only were material and money saved, but the quality of the work was guaranteed and the timetable kept.

In consequence, the Jenhochi safety operations were finished in time. The flood period was safely passed. And China had taken vast steps forward in planning, in technique, in far-sighted operations for the benefit of every man, woman, and child—vast steps forward in peaceful construction which will henceforth protect and benefit in this area alone one-seventh of all China's arable land.

CHINA'S NEW GREAT WALL

Traveling from Tientsin to the vast northeast, China's rapidly developing new industrial area, we reached the Great Wall of China, where it descends majestically from its 1,000-mile march along the mountaintops of northern China to the plains to meet the sea at Shukaikuan.

We rolled swiftly on in the fine new Chinese train, mountains receding to the west, broad and level plains stretching out before us northward; farmlands, farmlands as far as the eye could reach on either side of the track. Farmlands cultivated to the last inch, as usual, by China's industrious peasantry.

But what, we wondered, were those strong, short, hedge-like rows that ran at right angles to the railroad track? Now a couple, then a space; now a couple, then another space, and so on. Hedgerows, dividing fields, as in England? Too close for that, only alleys, not fields, between them. No; those hedge-like rows were baby forest trees, outposts of the vast shelter belts which will at length arrest the march of the Gobi Desert and change the climate of China.

Two thousand years ago, the Great Wall was built to save China from the devastation of nomads. But here begins a new Great Wall to save

China from the greater enemies of flood, famine, drought, and desiccating winds. The old wall remains a wonder of the world, though men still recall with pity the curses of the forced laborers who built it and with execration the name of the emperor who drove them to their task. The new wall will be a greater world wonder than the old, and will recall the enthusiasm, not the groans of its builders and the blessings, not the curses, on the name of its creator, Mao Tse-tung, who ushers in a new era of victory over nature, rather than over man.

There begins a new wall to save China from the greater enemies of flood famine drought and desicating winds.

Not long before seeing these new plantations, we had seen and flown over hundreds of miles of similar plantations in the south of Russia, plantations stretching on for thousands of miles in the broad Soviet lands, from southern Ukraine to the Urals, embracing an area larger than all Western Europe.

Five thousand miles away from China, those Russian forest shelter belts, running beside river beds and on the watersheds between them, planted round collective farm fields, ponds, and reservoirs, will break the dry winds, encourage richer vegetation, reduce evaporation, and change the climate of continental areas. Crops from the newly irrigated lands have been estimated at 8 million tons of wheat (more than the total wheat crop of China), 6 million tons of sugar beet (more than the total output of the United Kingdom), 3 million tons of cotton (more than the combined crop of Egypt and Pakistan), and half a million tons of rice.

That is the vision of Russia's fifteen-year plan of afforestation, with only eleven more to go. Already we have seen with our own eyes the fruits of four years' intensive work.

This vision has had, as it was bound to have, its repercussions on China. The new creative China presents precisely the same conditions and possibilities to meet precisely the same problems and difficulties that Russia faced. Hence on either side of the great Asian continent, 6,000 miles across, forests in right proportion, clothing valley and hills, will change climates, produce foodstuffs, industrial crops, and timber in unlimited quantities; the vast Asian mainland will burst into fertility and prosperity, and nourish in plenty the peace-loving peoples of the new world.

Mao Tse-tung, Chou En-lai, Chu Teh, Mo En-jo, together with all Chinese scientists and agronomists, saw the vision and sprang into action. Not a moment was lost. Like everything else in the new creative China, no sooner the thought than the deed; work begins at once.

The map of China's fifteen-year afforestation plan lies before me, together with the data of present achievement. Within thirty years forests will clothe over a million square miles of China's submarginal lands. Those barren hills of the Shantung Peninsula and those arid mountains in Kansu will delight the eye with entirely new landscapes. Chinese villages, roadsides, railsides, and mountainsides will be clad with green and studded with flowering, fruit-bearing trees.

Soviet experts estimate that 30 percent of forest land to other land is the correct proportion to meet the needs of weather protection and timber requirements. The Kuomintang, which had inherited a China with 10 percent of forest, had, together with Japanese vandalism, reduced this forest area to a bare 5 percent of the national territory. Forests in liberated China will, in thirty years' time, cover 20 percent of China's entire territory, with profound effects on climate and production. Brown denuded hills will become green. By cordial agreement with the farmers, various localities are being cordoned off, untouched by cattle or man, to expand with growth of shrubs and grasses and then with forest trees self-sown by natural propagation.

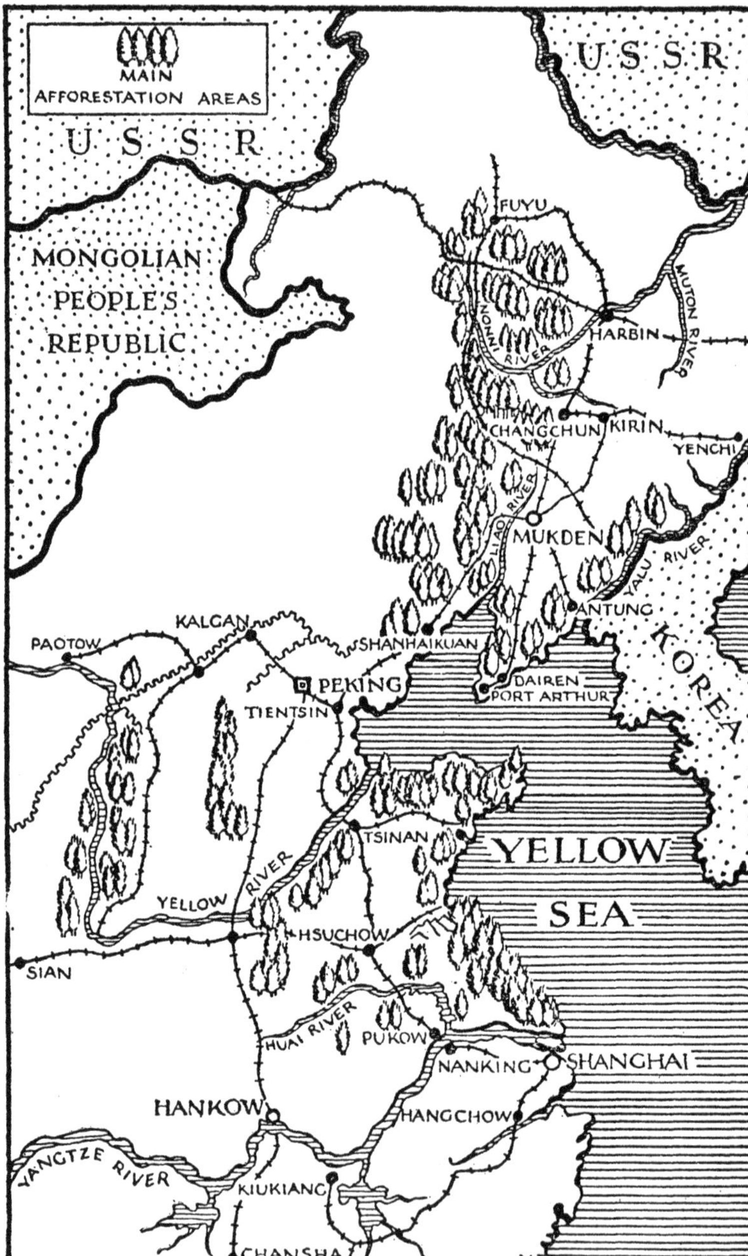
MAIN AFFORESTATION AREAS
U S S R
U S S R
MONGOLIAN PEOPLE'S REPUBLIC
FUYU
HARBIN
MUTON RIVER
NONNI RIVER
CHANGCHUN
KIRIN
YENCHI
LIAO RIVER
MUKDEN
YALU RIVER
ANTUNG
KOREA
KALGAN
PAOTOW
SHANHAIKUAN
PEKING
TIENTSIN
DAIREN
PORT ARTHUR
TSINAN
YELLOW SEA
YELLOW RIVER
HSUCHOW
SIAN
HUAI RIVER
PUKOW
NANKING
SHANGHAI
HANKOW
HANGCHOW
YANGTZE RIVER
KIUKIANG
CHANSHA
N.J.

China is a timber-starved land. Poverty, lack of coal fuel, and lack of transportation for it drove the peasants and others to strip bare what little was left of forest trees, of roadside trees, and of mountainside shrubs and grasses.

Twenty years ago I marveled at peasant skill, watching them cook with a minimum of implements. An old petrol can stuffed with wet clay, a narrow vertical hole from top to bottom, a narrow horizontal hole meeting it from one side, a scoop at the top to hold a saucer-shaped pan—and there you had the stove. A handful of coarse grass from the mountainside and there you had the fuel, fed stalk by stalk into the horizontal passage at the base. On that stove and with that fuel a peasant would cook a meal of rice or potatoes; or, if he could get it, of eggs, meat, and soup. That illustrated China's skill, but also China's poverty. And it explained China's denuded hillsides. Coal from China's mines and oil from China's oil wells and new money for their purchase all contribute to reclothe the mountainside.

On the road upward through Kanzu were the remnants of magnificent lines of giant willow trees which once gave shelter to dusty caravans. All that remains are gaunt trunks, barkless and dead, here and there a survivor to hint at the past. The roadside denuded, just as hillsides are denuded of shrubs and grases in search for fuel. Fresh trees now line the roads and are guarded as people's property by those who plant and own them.

The new transport facilities, diminished poverty, more understanding of the meaning of forests, together with a mighty willingness to back up the Government's determination to reclothe China with timber, enlist hundreds of thousands of willing hands to plant trees, rope off hills for natural propagation, and, under the inspiration of a new morality, to guard these precious elements of national riches from wanton or thoughtless destruction.

People begin to understand the meaning of floods, droughts, sandstorms, soil erosion, and other natural disasters, and how they may be fought and conquered.

Drought and sandstorms have year by year and century by century devastated the western and northern provinces of China. Soil erosion annually sweeps away 1,000 billion tons of silt from the Yangtze River basin alone; the Yellow River adds to the loss; together they produce the Yellow Sea, its turbid, ocher-colored waters stretching 100 miles out into the Pacific. All represent loss of rich earth, and most of it preventable loss.

The afforestation work, which will change all this, has been no sudden scheme, no mere flash in the pan. Though speedy in execution, it was carefully and deliberately thought out. The struggle for a tree-clad land had led to a scientific plan which in May, 1950, called for:

1. Enclosing approximately 2,900,000 hectares of forest land for natural propagation.
2. Collecting 1,812,413 kilograms of various kinds of seed for sowing and raising seedlings.
3. Raising 492,000,000 seedlings of various kinds in nurseries.
4. Planting trees in areas totaling approximately 120,000 hectares.

Great enthusiasm welcomed the program. Some 400 million trees were the target for 1950: the spring alone saw the target exceeded by three percent. Manchuria especially excelled; its target of 66 million trees was exceeded twice over. Tree-planting has become a dramatic mass campaign.

The core of the new planning is of course in the northlands and the great forest belts, which run parallel to the dykes along the shores of the Yellow River. Subsidiary belts, 360 miles long, abutting on the estuary of the Yangtze River in the south and girdling the coast as far as existing forests of the Yuntai Mountains in the north, will protect the east coast of China and the inland crops from violent eastern winds and the ocean typhoons, with the sea-water inundations which accompany them.

This latter scheme is scheduled for completion in 1958, to coincide with the completion of the great Huai River Control Scheme, both combined changing the face of nature in the central Chinese area and securing 7,700 square miles of good land for good crops, showing an output at least 50 percent greater than before, while the bare farms and villages of the countryside will burst with new beauties of willow, acacia, gingko, mulberry, cedar, and cypress.

In the north, planting of China's Great New Forest Wall will protect China's major industrial region against destructive desert winds. When planting is completed in the northeastern shelter belt, in ten years from now, 11,500 square miles of forest land will be the result. Forests will stretch 680 miles north and south, 190 miles across at the widest point. Seven thousand square miles now useless for agriculture, an area equal to one-third of the cultivated land of England, will be reclaimed, arid sections of northeastern China and Inner Mongolia will be green with meadows and golden with grain, and China will be blessed with a moist climate congenial to man and conducive to production.

No wonder we viewed with feelings of deep emotion these three-year-old hedge-like rows of trees near China's Great Wall when we learned the purpose they will serve.

The traveler to China in 1972 will look upon a Chinese landscape scarcely recognizable as that seen by us in 1952.

3 Learning to Live Together

EXPERIENCE TEACHES CO-OPERATION

THE land in China belongs to the men and women who till it. Nothing is likely to alter that fact in any foreseeable future. Each tiller is an owner. The only problem now remaining is how to till the land to the greatest advantage to both tiller and community. Is it best to till it in isolation or collectively?

Those who have studied collective farming in Russia and Eastern Europe have no hesitation in the answer. But those who say collectivize the agricultural land of China forthwith show small understanding of the Chinese situation. To the peasant it would appear that you were taking away with one hand what you gave with the other. And indeed, efficient collective farming is no easy occupation to be learned in a single day or a single year.

Furthermore, for the present even the isolated farmer is comparatively prosperous in comparison with his past poverty, with a small surplus instead of a large debt: for the moment he is content. Chinese individual farming is the most successful in the world. China has learned through millennia how to husband its soil; it understands compost and the return of human as well as animal manure to the land.

Another major factor also produces a peasant farmer's surplus—the return of that surplus which the landlord formerly took at the expense of peasant poverty. For the old feudal landlords had not, like the feudal landlords of tsarist Russia or Prussian Germany, used modern methods and modern machinery in the cultivation of their lands to produce a marketable surplus: a surplus, not sufficient indeed to supply the large-scale industry at which Russia, for her part, aimed, but large enough for the feudal order and to create a small body of rich men.

In China it was different. The feudal landlord had indeed a surplus for sale and for use in the towns. He even had a surplus for export. But that was not due to the economy of large-scale production. It was due to wringing the last grain of rice or wheat from the hungry, ill-clad, ill-housed peasant. That is the surplus which now passes to the peasant and leads to contentment.

Naturally, in such conditions the peasant could not and would not produce the maximum output possible. But since the radical land distribution has made him an owner and not a tenant at exorbitant rental, the peasant farmer produces more than formerly; the surplus that was wrung from him is now his own by right. He thus receives more, the town also receives more, and there is even more for export than was at first thought possible.

More, but by no means enough; for the demands of the town will grow as the scale of industrialization, already planned, grows. More, but not by any means up to the limits of possibility, if combination replaces isolation. The problem therefore is, and the necessity too, not only how to collectivize, but how to collectivize wisely, carrying the peasant willingly along with the process and not forcing it upon him heedlessly. China of all countries is capable of wise action of this kind, and will take no rash step to antagonize the peasant, whose gratitude is already immense, without whose help the liberation would never have come and without whose whole-hearted co-operation no collective farming is practicable.

Steps taken for this wise winning are already proving their value. They are threefold. First, get the peasant farmer familiar with the value of team work. Secondly, get him familiar with the development of team work in the consumers' and producers' co-operative societies. And thirdly, give him examples of successful collective farming, steps even now taken on a wider scale than many in the West realize. On ground now thoroughly and wisely prepared the second step preparatory to the final step is far advanced.

MUTUAL AID TEAMS

The growth of the mutual aid movement may be divided into two periods: that before and that after the Central People's Government had been set up in 1949. In the earlier period, when the People's Army was struggling against the Kuomintang, labor was short in the liberated areas: the men and women who were left on the farms, after the volunteers had joined the army or the partisans, had pooled their labor and carried on the struggle to keep up farm output despite shortage of workers under the slogan, "Organize to overcome difficulties." The mutual aid teams won their spurs by their contribution through organization to victory on the production front.

The second period, after the liberation, was a period of peace. With the return of men and the increase of draft animals agriculture was rehabilitated and the peasants had entered into a more prosperous life. But the value of mutual aid had been demonstrated and was eagerly applied to the nationwide reconstruction efforts which had already begun. New and self-explanatory slogans were launched: "Organize to increase yield, raise productivity, and improve livelihood"; "Improve technique to strengthen the mutual aid teams." Membership in mutual aid teams grew rapidly. In 1952, peasants who had joined mutual aid teams comprised more than 40 percent of the total peasantry in the whole country. In the old liberated areas such peasants amounted to 70 to 80 percent of the total.

The teams increased in popularity as their obvious benefits became apparent. We listened, for example, to the enthusiastic talk of an old but capable peasant farmer who was leader of one of these teams. Proudly exhibiting the small agricultural implements his team had already acquired, he described the increased harvest results which his team had shared. No single peasant of the divided estate could, at that time and in the general shortage so soon after the Japanese War and civil strife, afford more than the simplest tools and machinery and none could buy a mule. The half-dozen families in the peasant's team could, however, collectively, afford the small machines. They could also with great advantage divide the work among themselves, women as well as men, and concentrate all their labor strength upon one single task when necessity demanded it.

Types of mutual aid teams differ. There is the seasonal or temporary team, organized to make up seasonal or emergency shortages. These are less satisfactory; their mode of counting workdays is inexact and unstandardized.

The second type, all-the-year-round teams, are slower in growth, but greater in future prospects, and more just in their division of labor and counting of workdays on the principle of "equal pay for equal work."

All work in the best teams is now graded according to its nature, quality, and output, irrespective of the sex of the team member.

Teams of this second type purchase modern farm implements, waterwheels for irrigation and the like. They make life easier, enabling team members to undertake subsidiary tasks in order to supplement their income from agriculture. Their number increases year by year. In the six provinces of northeast China mutual aid teams in 1952 included some 70 percent of all rural families; about a quarter of these are of the all-the-year-round type.

The third type aims at uniting the various groups of the second type into a larger unit, enabling the purchase of machines for large-scale cultivation. Statistics for northeast China show that members in mutual aid teams get 30 percent more plowing done per man in a given period than the individual cultivator. Cotton yields on team-worked fields are 50 percent above those of families working separately.

The results of each type became both apparent and attractive: an increased share in the products at the year's end, with possibility of days off and holidays, made the benefit of the second and third types obvious, and after a year's or a couple of years' time neighboring peasants were clamoring for admission to the teams.

So the movement grew. It grows everywhere. And it receives due and eager support from the Government. There are "model" teams as well as "model" individual workers. That is, there are team groups of such outstanding achievement as entitle them to special recognition and reward. The team of peasants mentioned in an earlier paragraph was a model team. As a reward, it has been given a mule. With pride, the old man who spoke with us exhibited the gift. His were the only draft animals in the village.

It should also be observed that the mutual aid teams in no wise interfere with the direct ownership of the parcel of land allocated to each peasant at the great division. That parcel is still his parcel, his own individual parcel, which he cherishes as a long-desired and now happily acquired possession. What the team has done is to enable him to till his own parcel, not just with the aid of this or that neighbor, but with the whole organized assistance of a team to aid him in any emergency whatsoever.

No wonder the team movement grows.

A big contributary agent in preparing the ground for further agricultural advance along collective lines, working side by side with the mutual aid movement, is provided by the great construction works. As we gazed upon the multitudes operating on the Chinkiang Water Project—they numbered 300,000—and observed the colossal organization and the fruits of it, we saw at once the value of this object lesson in mass teamwork. Powerless had been the work of local dyke-builders, powerless the work of the most powerful feudal lords, powerless the work of the whole province to give protection against the middle Yangtze floods which had been the agelong quest of every Chinese farmer in the flood-threatened areas.

Contrast this with the all-powerful operation of the teamwork of a whole nation. Could there be a wider advertisement for teamwork?

The bulk of the workers on the Yangtze Project and other projects were farmers, gathered voluntarily from all the threatened districts around—farmers receiving pay for their work, with security as the final great reward. These farmers, returning home to their respective villages, carried with them the overwhelming vision they had seen, and with it the recollection of their own small but essential share in the project.

That vision would be translated in village after village and hamlet after hamlet into graphic tales of the work: this team digging and excavating, that team preparing foundations for immense sluice structures; this team stone-facing the dykes, that team erecting the huge piers to carry the sluice gates; another assembling the steel gates themselves, yet another erecting them; some teams building temporary shelters, others laying electric power cables, others managing the commissary, others equipped with hospitals and nurses to give first and second aid in case of accident, and yet others, skilled actors and sweet-voiced singers, to entertain the peasants when tired after the long day's work.

Who can estimate the value of this drama of teamwork? Indeed, by such vast construction, the psychological groundwork of a whole nation is being prepared for teamwork, collective enterprise. Results so dramatic, so speedy—the Chungking-Chengfu Railway completed and the middle Yangtze made secure by the vast Chinkiang flood project, both opened in the same months of this year of 1952, the one after some two years' work, the other after less than three months—leave an indelible impression on all minds. Wise guidance and detailed instruction alone are needed to drive the lesson home and teach the inner meaning of the principle here applied on so vast a scale, of winning each "to work according to his capacity in order that each may receive according to need." All giving technical skill, laboring strength, organizing ability, or artistic and musical gifts; all receiving urgently needed security, as on the small scale through their own farm team, so now on the large scale in safety of life and property.

CO-OPERATIVES IN NEW CHINA

June, 1949, 13,466,887 members in Chinese co-ops; June, 1950, 20,176,448 members; June, 1951, 51,000,000 members; August, 1952, 106,000,000 members.

Never was seen so phenomenal a growth in any other co-operative movement in the world, or indeed in any movement of any kind before; from 13 million to 106 million members in three years. No country in the world can equal, let alone surpass that record.

We can only explain it when we understand the new demands arising from the new Land Liberation Laws, giving for the first time to multitudes of men and women their own land with all its resources, and also all its needs and responsibilities, for their own use.

Ownership of land needs cash or credit to equip it and work it to advantage. The peasants lacked both. What must they do? Let Lao Wang, a peasant farmer, state his own solution:

"We needed loans to get going, fertilizers for the land, food to get us through till harvest. We could raise them at the co-op, because the co-op could raise money from the banks or the city co-op. When the co-op first started last year we had loans from it, interest free. That made people believe in it. In the old days where would we peasants go for loans? To the merchants or the landlords. And what would we pay in interest? Anything up to a third of the loan. There wasn't one of us who didn't want a co-op loan. Who wouldn't when interest is never higher than 2 percent? Everyone took at least a *picul* of bean-cake to fertilize the land. Some of us have 250 *catties* laid down this year, where once we only put 150 or less. Though the land's good, crops were never so big in the old days. We'd get one, or one and a half, perhaps 2 *piculs* of rice out of every *mou,* for as long as I can remember. This year we're getting two and a half."

There were other inducements to membership. Lao Wang's farm lay in a district where the major crop was rice. But rice, looking much like wheat, needs, like wheat, shaking from the husks, formerly an arduous process. Then came the "huller," or small threshing machine, too expensive for peasant purchase and generally loaned by city merchants at high rentals to yield high profits. The co-operatives bought a huller, rented it generally and for no profit at all, merely for working expenses and replacement expenses. Should, however, any small profit be made, that went into a reserve fund to finance subsidiary enterprises; it was not distributed as dividend. Dividends are not popular in Chinese co-operatives. Surplus money is plowed back into some new enterprise.

For instance, in Lao Wang's district the co-operatives started a "rope-walk." Members and shareholders thought this a necessary and profitable sideline in which to invest any surplus money left over after they paid for food, clothing, and equipment.

Next came the perennial problem of marketing the crop to the best advantage. This brought before the farmer another side of the co-operative's activities. Not only could the co-operative supply loans, machinery, and fertilizers at low cost, because seeking no profit and cutting out the middleman, the co-operative could also sell the product at the most advantageous rates in the city. Indeed, co-operatives tend to displace the profit-taking middleman altogether. The co-operative could sell direct to the factory, which in turn made the consumer goods with which to stock the village co-operative store. And when factory workers needed food and raw materials, the village, through the co-operative store, could supply them—another inducement to the farmers to join the co-operatives.

As the product increased, the money in the peasant's pocket increased. What more natural, therefore, than to make day-to-day purchases at the co-operative stores, which cuts out the middleman's profit entirely and brings the shop to the peasant's door. It is both cheaper and more convenient for peasants to buy at the nearby village co-operative shop than to journey to the town and swell the merchants' profits.

I watched peasants buying in just such a village shop. No smart co-operative establishment such as you may see in any English town. Just a crowded village shop like the small shops in the Scottish highlands or Welsh villages of my youth; small general-purpose stores, stocked with everything salable. So in the Chinese village co-operative store you will see tea, vinegar, soap, notebooks, salt, flour, cloth by the yard or in ready-made suits, bicycles, cigarettes—all cheaper than in the merchants' shops.

What you find in one village co-operative store is repeated in hundreds of thousands of similar village co-operatives. They are products of an activity which sprang spontaneously from the people themselves and is cordially welcomed by the Liberation Government, which sees and rightly sees in the co-operative movement, correctly and efficiently run, an invaluable step on the road to socialism. Article 29 of China's *Common Program* puts it plainly:

"Co-operative economy is of a semi-socialist nature and is an important component of the people's economy as a whole. The People's Government shall foster its development and accord it preferential treatment."

Consequently, consumer and marketing co-operatives are sedulously fostered in all ways, state-owned trading organizations supplying them with low-priced commodities and giving them priority in the purchase of farm products. Low-interest loans are issued from State banks, with tax rebates of 20 percent as compared with other enterprises. Reduced charges are levied on farm insurance.

Co-operatives in return aid the State organizations, serving as a link between the state economy and the scattered individual economies of peasants and handicraftsmen that form their membership. Again, as it is the duty of the State to keep a balance between agricultural and industrial production and at the same time to increase both, it must keep prices stable. To do this planning is essential. There must be enough goods and raw materials for the towns and enough town-made consumers' goods for the country. Co-operatives insure both. In touch with all the scattered units of the countryside and of the town, they gather information essential for plan-making and encourage the members to carry out their share of the over-all State plans.

Since the northeast has been liberated longest, it is there that the swing to the co-operative has become more pronounced. In the northeast 85 percent of the total value of industrial goods distributed by State trading organizations finds its way to the people through the co-operatives; 69 percent of grain and other raw materials returns to the State through the co-operatives; town co-operatives get flour, sugar, cloth, cereals, coal, etc., at prices from 7 to 12 percent lower than those prevailing at the time.

Producers' co-operatives have naturally grown more slowly than consumers' co-operatives, which catered for immediate and obvious needs. They embrace both handicraftsmen and farm producers, the former being organized according to trades, such as rug-making, shoe-making, cloth-weaving. The producers' co-operatives market the goods and in return supply the necessary raw materials for their manufacture. They also advise on improvements in technique.

Some agricultural or farming co-operatives have been organized directly by the local peasants to increase output through the pooling of land, labor, farm equipment, and capital. They have proved the success of these co-operatives to their neighbors, and further development is only limited by the supply of machines and equipment and trained cadres. While awaiting machines, the main effort toward collectivization at the moment must take the form of creating successful mutual aid teams. All this nationwide ramification of co-operatives through county, provincial, and administrative area federations is co-ordinated through the All-China Federation of Co-operatives, which was established in June, 1950, at the First National Congress of Co-operative Workers.

The co-operative movement not only improves the members' livelihood, it serves as a great school of democratic organization and a training ground for cadres among the mass of peasants and workers. Is has shown the small agricultural producers who compose the overwhelming mass of the Chinese people the concrete path of advance that will end the days of poverty for ever and build up a strong, rich, and prosperous people's state.

CHINA'S PIONEER COLLECTIVE FARM

On the steppe, fifteen miles east of Chiamussu, on the south bank of the Sungari River in Sungkiang Province, away up in northeast China, there is being conducted with all the care that such a demonstration demands China's first collective farm. Much hangs on the failure or success of Hsinghuo Farm—"Spark Farm" it is called—as to whether it will be a spark setting light to a trail of similar farms which might run like a prairie fire far and wide through China's vast territories, or whether it will be snuffed out as a failure.

Should it fail, that may prolong for decades the existence of the present agricultural system which is better indeed than its feudal predecessor, yet operates far below the potential production of China's rich and far-spreading lands. The "spark farm" must be successful and demonstrably successful before China's farmers are encouraged to raise their so-newly-won landownership from individual to collective ownership.

The demonstration is happily proving highly successful. That can now be said at the outset. And its success gives it widespread publicity. That in itself guarantees that the success is real, for what is widely publicized can be widely criticized.

The Hsinghuo collective farm is an admirable demonstration of large-scale modern socialist agriculture. It began in 1947 when the Communist

Party and the Government decided to establish a model farming community on the grasslands east of Chiamussu. Peasants who joined were given land, houses, implements—all things essential to insure success to a collective farm, planned on a large scale.

Difficulties were only to be expected. The leaders lacked experience. They made mistakes. They first divided the land among working groups of four families each. This was a step in the wrong direction, for the peasants quickly dropped into their old stride of isolated farming, and the family groups partitioned out the land among themselves. They were back in the old grooves. And even where land was not partitioned there was shirking and striving after bigger shares of the harvest. The result was poor. The rice yield of 2,360 kilograms per hectare, despite good rainfall, was inadequate.

The lesson of the failure was quickly learned. Education—political education—was intensified in 1948 to overcome the selfish smallholder outlook. The principle of voluntary mutual aid was inculcated. In 1949 three different types of organization were tried out. Some of the more backward peasants preferred their own isolated plots, the great majority formed small mutual aid teams, while some formed farming groups on the model of producers' co-operatives.

One such group, composed of five families working as an agricultural producers' co-operative, achieved the best result and became the precursor of the present "Spark" collective farm, led by Chin Pai-shan. Their yield despite the insect pests of 1949, was high: it reached 2,400 kilograms per hectare, or, on land not affected by pests, as much as 3,200 kilograms. Labor efficiency had advanced, and the average area now cultivated by each working member was 1.7 hectares as compared with one hectare in 1948. They were elected as the model group.

Two further difficulties arose. The co-operative harvest was not distributed, as Chairman Chin had recommended, according to the amount of actual work done by each member. The division was according to the land subscribed. That handicapped the hard workers. For example, the Chairman's family was small, only his wife and himself. Both worked hard and exceeded their norms by forty workdays a year. Had payment been made on workdays, instead of land shares, they would have got 700 kilograms of grain, instead of the 400 kilograms they actually received. This was a threat to labor enthusiasm.

Another difficulty was the shortage of work hands, demanding, as it were, a labor reservoir from which to dispatch particular workers or specialists to work in different places whenever they are needed.

The group, in consequence, turned itself into a collective, distributing the fruits of joint labor on the basis of workdays only. Membership of the group expanded.

The whole farming community of which this group was a unit grew deeply interested: almost all the peasants applied for membership in the group. So in 1950 a collective farming group of fourteen families was formed, and the distributive system of "to each according to his labor" applied. The larger unit made possible the provision of a shock force for busy seasons, or for emergencies, such as the eradication of insect pests.

The result was highly satisfactory. The average area cultivated by each member rose to 1.8 hectares and the yield to 3,400 kilograms per hectare, the highest ever recorded in those parts. Indicative of the success, the membership quickly rose to thirty-six families.

All this is soon stated. It was not soon or easily achieved. Its achievement demanded intensive political, economic, and social education of the peasants. The voluntary principle was never violated: members and non-members alike had access to land.

In order to speed up the work of this vital experimental farm the Government advanced a loan to purchase forty oxen and many farming implements.

The farm prospered. It has achieved its target. It not only provides for its members substantial quantities of grain and other produce as recompense for their workdays, but has also sent donations of grain and hay to the Chinese Volunteers fighting in Korea and made allowances to the families with sons fighting.

A large surplus remains, even after payment for and provision of 12 to 15 percent for expanding production and purchase of modern machinery.

The amenities are greatly in excess of anything the isolated peasant could possibly secure; a newly-built house with wide windows and electric light, good food, books and newspapers, new clothes, boots and gloves.

The story is told of Chiang Ching-hsaio, who came to the farm in 1948 clothed in rags. Next year he joined the model group, and now as a member of the "Spark" collective farm his earnings are ten times what they were in 1948. He and his family have bought thirty suits of clothing in two years, three new sets of bedding, new books and magazines. They eat rice, and no longer the coarser grains of their previous diet.

A new school, nursery, co-operative stores, and a club were the targets for 1952.

One element of economy and one personal boon arising from the collective farm system is sometimes overlooked. It enables each individual to be more fully himself, to develop along the lines of his own special tastes and aptitudes. While all are able to acquire some mastery of the principles of mechanism, so also all acquire an understanding of the practical principles of plowing, digging, sowing, and reaping and the principles of animal husbandry. Thus equipped, the individuals can share the common task with greater regard for their various tastes and aptitudes.

CHINA'S MULTINATIONAL FAMILY

Ninety percent of China's multinational family are Hans, whom we speak of as Chinese. The remaining 10 percent amounting to some 40 million or more, include at least sixty different nationalities, living mainly in the vast regions—half the area of the whole country—along the borderlands of China.

The history of these minorities has been dark. Take Tibet, always regarded as a Chinese province and Tibetans as a minority group within it. When I visited Tibet and went to the Butter Festival at Sining in 1932 the Han traders were ruthless. The Han people, particularly the Kuomintang, treated the Tibetans with supercilious contempt. Rewi Alley recalls the day when some Tibetans came over to see his school in Sandan. The local magistrate of Sandan, visiting the school at the same time, swore at the Tibetans and ordered his guard to drive them away as though they were dogs.

This attitude was fostered by the imperialists, who welcomed national feuds as likely to soften up the whole country for invasion.

Today the Tibetans are treated with respect. The Liberation Army, struggling against the Kuomintang, took nothing from the Tibetans, rather giving them technical assistance in agriculture and medical aid, showing respect for their human dignity and national customs, and thus tying the Tibetans the more closely to China and to the other nationalities which occupy the fringe areas. The minority peoples had quickly learned to distinguish between the Kuomintang Army and the Communist Army.

Pillaged, oppressed, and often massacred or removed wholesale from one area to another, the population of the minority peoples had shrunk under the Kuomintang rule; their production had dwindled. All were living below their possibilities.

The present policy is to wipe out inherited inequalities. The Common Program obliges the People's Government to "assist the masses of the people of all the national minorities to develop their political, economic, cultural, and educational construction."

The isolation of the minorities, pushed formerly into inaccessible and desolate regions, has ceased. Three large delegations have made extensive tours in the minority areas, south, southwest, and north, since 1950, to discuss local problems and to help economically, culturally and medically. Delegates of the national minorities have been welcomed in Peking. At the end of 1951 delegates from thirty-nine minorities took part in an enlarged conference of the General Committee for Nationalities in Peking. "Now we have Chairman Mao, none dare bully us again."

National equality cannot be real without democratic self-government. The minorities, that is, must be masters of their own home affairs. The Common Program laid down regional autonomy as a fundamental policy of the Central People's Government. One hundred and thirteen national autonomous regions have come into being, and in regions where different nationalities live together 165 democratic united governments have been set up.

This new self-government has been received with boundless enthusiasm: "Isn't it wonderful that such a thing can happen? . . . In the past none of us could get a job in even the lowest category; now we have our own government."

Political freedom and self-government are speedily followed by economic and cultural development, by which alone equality of rights becomes equality of actual condition.

This is no easy task, for most of the minority localities were poorly adapted for agricultural production. They needed help and technical knowledge from their richer Han neighbors. Instead, they got extortion. The Tibetans had to pay one ounce of gold for 20 pounds of tea. At Sining, the Tibetan town where I stayed in 1952, Tibetan shepherds would get only 140 pounds of wheat for 100 pounds of wool. Now they get 640 pounds of wheat, or if they wish to exchange wool for cotton cloth, they get fourteen and a half times as much as before the Liberation.

These figures speak for themselves. The minority nationalities naturally show gratitude: Greater China becomes ever more closely knit together.

The process develops rapidly and extends to far-distant areas. Pack teams carry commodities into the remotest mountains from 750 State trading points. Purchases of wool and medicinal herbs went up between two and three times in a single year. Minority nationalities in the northwest get from twice to several dozen times as much money for individual products as before the Liberation. The standard of living advances. Equality of condition comes nearer.

Industrial raw materials, animal products, wool, and the like make up somewhat for lack of first-class agricultural land. Inner Mongolia has coal and salt; Sinkiang petroleum and non-ferrous metals; the southwest copper, tung oil, asbestos, mica, and camphor. With the incubus of imperial capitalism removed, these native resources are rapidly developed.

Rampant diseases, bubonic plague, malaria, syphilis, are resolutely attacked. To combat disease, the Ministry of Health of the Central Govenment has already organized eight anti-epidemic groups to work in minority regions. Local medical groups and clinics follow. Remarkable are the results. In the year before the liberation 13,000 people died of bubonic plague in Inner Mongolia: in 1950 only seventeen.

Cultural backwardness presents numerous problems. Many minorities have no written language, and many that have, such as Tibetans and Mongolians, have no vocabulary for present-day needs. To meet these emergencies, books were rapidly printed in the Mongolian, Tibetan, and Uighur languages, new written languages being created where non-existent before. The Yi nationality borders on the wealthy Szechuan Province, and is testing a Latinized written language.

Public education in Inner Mongolia has made great strides since my last visit in 1932.

A special Academy in Peking gives courses of training for leadership for cadres from national minorities. Such cadre education is sought as eagerly today as the forced education of a minority of youth to exploit their own people on behalf of reactionary Chinese governments was resisted formerly.

China's 40 million people of minority nationalities are awake and on the move, a joy to themselves, a strength to China, and a reinforcement to the peace forces of the world.

PART II. THE NEW LIFE AND ITS PHYSICAL BASIS

1 The Battle for Health

WELL-NIGH bottom in the list of health-conscious nations a decade ago, China has sprung with one bound to a premier place. Her inheritance of ill-health is her major problem. It has been estimated that 100 million people—one in five—are in need of medical aid in some shape or form, the bitter fruit of centuries of oppression, of imperialist exploitation, of feudalism, of man-made calamities, of low living standards, of inadequate health aids and precautions, and of unchecked and devastating epidemics. A land of filth and superstition; a land of flies, mosquitoes, bugs, and rats; a land devoid of sanitation, ignorant of the laws of health; a land with a monstrous death rate, with a shocking and truly appalling infant mortality rate, rising at times to 250 deaths per 1,000 births—that was China as the Kuomintang left it and as the Liberation government found it.

The Kuomintang took no drastic steps in the conquest of disease: they left China worse than they found it.

Liberated China, on the other hand, attacked the enemies of health no less resolutely than flood, drought, and famine. Attacked them with scientific skill and sound common sense. Enlisted the popular will behind a nationwide campaign for positive health, depending not merely upon a handful of trained cadres—the technical name in China for trained government executives—and highly qualified doctors, but supplying trained cadres as officers in a nationwide army of health workers which would bring all enemies of health within range of its attack and enlist all workers, even boys and girls, even small children, in its scope of scientific method. A task tackled with singular skill and imagination.

Frontal attack alone was useless. To provide doctors and hospitals adequate for 100 million patients was impossible within decades. The effort, indeed, to provide adequate and skilled health personnel was, as we shall see, not left out of account; but additional work of supreme value was done, and done at once. Disease was sidetracked, the foe met and defeated before it reached its human victim. And it was just here that all, even children, could join the fighting ranks.

On the street, one day, we passed a small boy of five or six. He held in his hand a tightly-corked bottle, half full of dead flies; his day's quota in the fight.

In the plague-infested areas you very often see a deep trench with sheer sides, surrounding a city or village. Up to it march boys and girls with spears, adorned with gay red tassels. The ditch is a rat-trap. The boys and girls are the extermination squad. No rat can enter or leave the city without traversing the trench whose steep, unclimbable walls make it a death-trap. Rats carry plague-lice. To kill rats is to kill plague. In north-east China 35 million rats were killed in 1951 and 10 million in the spring of 1952—40 million rats were killed in one year. And in the same year 6 million dwellers in the plague areas received anti-plague inoculation. From January to June, 1951, the number of plague cases was 80 percent below the same period for 1950. A war against rodents unparalleled anywhere in the world.

It was the same with cholera. In the last two years over 30 million people in the potential cholera areas have been inoculated against the disease; there has been no case of cholera in the past three years.

The same again with kala-azar, a health problem of long standing and with schistosomiasis—the one due to sand-flies and the other to snails; each levying a heavy toll on life and health in China. One champion killer of disease-bearing snails destroyed 400 of them in a single hour.

In Peking and other great cities there has been a complete elimination of stray dogs which were suspected of being reservoirs of encephalitis virus and many infections. On the street walls in Nanking, in Canton, in Peking, or in far-northerly Fushan, indeed everywhere, north, south, east, and west, you may see gaily-painted dramatic pictures of the war against the Five Enemies of Health—flies, mosquitoes, mosquito larvæ, bugs, and rats. Slogans abound—"Everybody needs health," "To protect the health of the people is the people's duty"—in order to enlist a nation-wide army for a pest-proof China. The small boy we met with his trophy of flies had seen the poster, had begged a bottle, and had collected his daily quota.

Additional posters tell you how to clean your home and clothes, how to handle children, etc. A constant flow of radio instructions drive these lessons home and newspapers carry frequent articles on health.

In Canton, in a building where once Mao Tse-tung had taught, a building now used as a kindergarten for small children, I watched a group of small boys and girls singing. At the end of each verse they all lifted their right hands and stabbed their left arms—a vaccination song. The whole nation has become vaccination-minded. Before the Liberation, vaccination against smallpox was sparse and inefficient, the largest number of persons vaccinated in one year (1946) being no more than 7.6 million. But in three years since the Liberation 307 million people have been vaccinated, and the disease has almost been entirely eliminated.

To achieve these results was no easy task: it demanded widespread and resolute attack. The masses were ignorant. They lacked instruction. Campaigns wisely began as far as possible with teachers and schools. In Chishiang County, for instance, in Pingyuan Province, Mi Pao-yin, a woman teacher, had been elected as Model Health Worker for 1951. At the Primary School Teachers' Conference she mobilized her fellow teachers to fight against smallpox. In her own school she had instructed her children in vaccination, sending them subsequently to instruct their parents. She followed this up with a house-to-house visitation. Within one month she had personally vaccinated 3,202 neighbors, in addition to her entire school of 226 pupils. People from nearby villages lined up for their turn.

Miss Mi is an accomplished musician. Enlisting her art in the campaign, she has composed thirty-four songs on health topics, exposing harmful and obstructive superstitions and describing the symptoms and dangers of common diseases. She writes health plays and trains her children to act them.

Some districts experience more difficulties than others and need exceptional measures. In Linhsien County, for instance, through sheer conservatism and distrust of anything new, the smallpox vaccination campaign had begun to hang fire. Dr. Ko, the medical officer, called a meeting in his own village, explained the benefits and reasons for vaccination. Then, bringing his own children and grandchildren onto the platform, he vaccinated them in full view of the people. The campaign had no further difficulties in Dr. Ko's area.

The attack upon flies, mosquitoes, and bugs is also resolute and sustained. The International Scientific Commission reported that already in the summer of 1952 they noted the great cleanliness and order in the streets, parks, yards, and shops of Peking and the complete absence of mosquitoes and almost complete absence of flies.

Side by side with this campaign against insect pests and rats, goes the campaign for all-round cleanliness of houses, streets, villages, and towns. Dirt is the breeding-ground of disease. Dirt must be removed. The attack upon dirt at times reaches epic proportions. A 202,638-ton heap of pestilential rubbish in Peking, an age-long accumulation, was removed by 73,537 voluntary workers. Thirty-five thousand cartloads and 800 truckloads were moved. In 1950, 500,000 cubic meters of rubbish were removed; in 1951, 700,000 cubic meters.

Even more dramatic was the cleaning of Peking's notorious "Dragon Beard Ditch."

In the Peking I knew in 1932, this vast open sewer wound its filthy way behind the famous Temple of Heaven. Never was more dramatic contrast, Temple and sewer. Few buildings fashioned by man compare with the chaste and sublime beauty of Peking's Temple of Heaven, a masterly composition, its great marble platforms enclosed by carved marble balustrades, aged to the semblance of old ivory, rising tier upon tier beneath an azure sky, nothing else visible except tree-tops and far horizons.

And there, just beyond those trees, which severed it from the Temple's transcendent beauty, ran this pestilential ditch, the menace of 300 years—stagnant, filled with garbage, rotting matter, dead dogs and cats, the haunt of sewer rats and loathsome worms, the breeding-ground of flies, beetles, and mosquitoes, the seed-ground of pestilence. Never did heaven and hell exist in such close proximity.

Thank God, the "Dragon Beard Ditch" has gone. The Kuomintang never touched it. The Liberation Government laid eager hands on it at once; voluntary hands, people's hands. The ditch was cleared and cleaned. Five miles of concrete conduits carry away the sewage beneath a clean concrete road. Piped water was introduced for the first time into the little houses which line its course: running water is now available for the entire population. An old inhabitant exclaimed: "I have been here for seventy-two years, but this is the first year I have lived in a clean place, with no flies and no mosquitoes or worms to trouble me."

The dramatic cleansing of the "Dragon Beard Ditch" was too great an opportunity for Chinese poets and dramatists to let pass untold or unsung. The famous playwright Lao Sheh made it the theme of a play so moving that it travels in theater form and film form from end to end of China, firing the admiration and emulation of millions. Other towns follow suit: 12,000 tons of rubbish have been cleared from Changsha, the town I visited twice, and new main sewers laid. A lovely flowered square replaces the old putrid dump in another town. Tientsin is laying 200 kilometers of new sewer drains.

It is not, however, enough to cleanse towns in general. Cleanliness must rule everywhere and be maintained. Streets and houses must be kept at a high level of cleanliness. In Peking each street has it own sanitary committee, usually one person to every ten houses or families, to inspect the houses and yards, to advise and to warn. Dust-bins must be emptied, accumulations of dirt removed, and so forth. Even holes in trees are sealed with a mixture of clay and lime, to kill mosquito larvæ breeding after the rain.

The quest for cleanliness is popular and spreads everywhere. Whitewashed wooden garbage boxes with lids stand outside every house in many villages. I spent a Sunday in Pengpu, formerly a dirty railway junction town, now the headquarters of the Huai River Project. In the afternoon we passed a troop of teen agers, led by a band and gay with red silk banners—silk is a lovely material for banners, floating and waving in soft and graceful curves: they were voluntary health squads, out to secure a clean city. It was the middle of June. We slept undisturbed in the heart of the city without mosquito nets and beneath wide-open windows.

It would be a mistake to suppose that the new health spirit and the new health measures arose straight out of the blue at the time of the Liberation in 1949. They had an earlier history. The Liberation Army had, from very small beginnings, been building up a medical service, sanitary, simple, scientific, and efficient, which grew as the army grew, until at length it served five million men and spread its example in each liberated locality.

Naturally, medical work attains high efficiency in the great river control constructions, where hundreds of thousands of men and women, collected from far-scattered villages and towns, live for months in close proximity and in temporary dwellings.

Formerly such assemblies gave rise to epidemics and widespread sickness. No epidemic nor any outbreak of sickness arose at the Middle Yangtze or the Huai River Control Constructions: high efficiency in sickness control, in mass health education and sanitation kept epidemics at bay. Such camps are a very school for health. Every peasant returning from the great constructions goes home with knowledge of modern sanitation: latrines, well placed and clean; water, pure and plentiful; food, wholesome and well cooked; incitements everywhere to personal cleanliness, and daily lectures on the nature and value of means to health. The more impressive through the excessive simplicity of the means used; nothing beyond the reach of an ordinary argricultural village and its carpenter's shop. Only one percent of China's population own water closets, the vast majority use earth closets, simple, straightforward, and clean.

Construction camps, besides being admirable schools of mutual aid and collective enterprise, are an aid to personal cleanliness and public sanitation. They do for country folk what the towns seek for the unsanitary, overcrowded areas inherited from a ruthless past. A quarter of a million dwellers in a poor area of Canton, formerly without pure water supply or lavatory accommodation, public or private, now receive pure water from hydrants, and have for their use 100 public lavatories. Riverside sampans also enjoy fresh water from hydrants, no longer obliged to drink from the Pearl River, into which they empty their sewage.

Railway trains are scrupulously clean, and I even saw food-sellers at wayside stations dressed in white overalls and wearing face-masks. Tea, which is provided free for all, is served in covered glass containers. Trains from the north are scrupulously disinfected.

The Kuomintang did nothing drastic about medical aid or conquest of disease, formulated no systematic health service, rested content with a shocking minimum of doctors, outrageously concentrated in a few major towns, leaving vast areas beyond the reach of any type of medical aid. Sinkiang Province, double the area of France, possessed only fifteen qualified doctors; the mass of the people, unserved by scientific medicine, were left to the questionable mercy of folk-herbalists, old midwives' fancies, and innumerable superstitious practices. Modern medicine was not for the masses, only for the well-to-do. As with everything else, deprived of paved roads, running water, electric light, and other modern amenities, the poor, even in Shanghai, had little or no access to modern medical practice. They were left to sicknes, fate, or death.

China suffers and will long suffer from a grievous shortage of modern doctors and surgeons—an appalling hangover from the past. There are indeed native Chinese doctors, and surgeons too, 180,000 of them; not enough, and ill-equipped with modern knowledge and antiseptic methods. One warm Sunday afternoon in the springtime of 1932 I watched a Chinese surgical operation in Youchow. It took place in the sunshine and on the roadside. Boils were the trouble. The surgeon laid his instruments on a small table, lit a spirit lamp and boiled a few drops of water in a test-tube. Emptying the water swiftly, he deftly placed the steam-filled tube mouth upwards around the edge of the boil. Steam cooled. A vacuum was formed; the pus sucked out. Most scientific. The surgeon then took a pad, passed his manipulating tools through the flame, smartly removed the tube, scraped the wound and clapped on the pad to cover it. But not before he had spat on the wound.

China's 180,000 native doctors undeniably need retraining. In the main, I believe, they welcome it. But it is wisely planned, as is Chinese training in general. Though many of China's leading doctors and surgeons are Western-trained, there is a revolt in Chinese medical circles against implicit faith in America's medical science. Not everything Chinese was bad, and China is developing her own medical science and can count on many able men to aid her. China's Western-trained medical scientists strive to keep an open mind, to examine and employ any method, Eastern or Western, that offers good empirical results, but never neglecting the quest of a scientific explanation of the success.

It is rightly thought that foreign methods cannot be transplanted wholesale and without modification onto Chinese soil. The whole situation must be carefully weighed. And this cannot be done in the study or the isolated laboratory. It demands immersion in Chinese life to understand and develop methods appropriate to Chinese psychology and conditions. Medical and surgical re-education is needed; "reformed thought" is needed, as well by foreign-trained doctors and surgeons as by the old-time Chinese doctor. The latter needs to learn some of the broad principles of scientific medicine and surgery, principles applicable at all times, and in all lands—for example, principles of anatomy and circulation, principles of sterilization and manipulative surgery.

The modern surgeon also needs to learn and can do so. The former tension between old and new can be and is being resolved. It had become serious. The new had no use for old-time medicine and drugs, etc., and would banish all. The old, knowing the empirical value of such things, rejected those who despised them and the methods they employed. This tension lessens today under the new reformed thought. The foreign-trained doctor learns the much-needed lesson that whereas a really scientific mind should be, and will be, doubtful and critical, it should also be willing to try any methods that achieve results, willing to experiment perpetually, and ready to learn that true scientists will not reject any method yielding good results.

One example of Chinese willingness to practice new processes which in other lands, whether in the West or in the Soviet Union, have given new and surprisingly good results is the treatment known as "tissue serum therapy." Filatov, the famous Russian eye specialist, had made an interesting discovery when, for lack of a living eye, or one only just dead, he had, in an emergency, used a cornea which had been severed some time back from a living body and preserved at a low temperature. He discovered that it served even better than fresh tissue. Some process had taken place during the low-temperature period, some development in reaction to the new conditions within the still living tissue, which gave it new curative powers. Trying this same method, extremely simple in practice, in cases of asthma and many other conditions, he achieved excellent results. A friend of mine in Peking suffered from deafness. Immediate improvement followed tissue grafting.

Many practitioners in China have used the method, among them my own nephew and his wife, while serving as missionary doctors in Szechuan. Tissue grafting is now practiced in numerous Chinese medical centers, and for many diseases.

The shortage of trained medical personnel is met in various ways. For economy of manpower, training is divided into three grades: (1) university grade, with a five-year course; (2) middle grade, with a two-year course; (3) elementary grade, with a six-month or one-year course. Grades 2 and 3 include nursing in all its branches.

To speed up training in the medical schools, historical matter is shortened, lectures are brought into closer relation to practice, stress being laid on important matters in practice.

The training of midwives is an immediate problem. The experience of midwife Wang Chi-ying of Linhsien, Pingyuan Province, illustrates it. A woman of forty-five with bound feet—daughter, granddaughter, and great-granddaughter of midwives—Miss Wang was typical of the past;

she regularly lost more than half of her deliveries with tetanus convulsions. With some hesitation, she consented to retrain. Becoming a model student, she asked pathetically: "Why was I not told of this before? How many children have died through my ignorance?" Since completing her course, midwife Wang Chi-ying has delivered forty-three babies without a single loss.

In 1950 alone 46,371 old-style midwives were retrained with thorough understanding of sterilization and asepsis. By the end of 1957 every administrative village will possess at least one modern-trained midwife.

This re-education of midwives has lowered the infant mortality rate from tetanus by one third between 1949 and 1951; infant mortality as a whole and maternal mortality were reduced by one-half in the same period.

Medical equipment for the whole of China is a formidable proposition, but great progress has been made in the organization and productive capacity of the laboratories providing vaccines and serums. After two years of hard work China has become able to produce 48 percent of her pharmaceuticals and general medical equipment. The manufacture of both proceed rapidly, the goal being complete self-sufficiency in 1952 in sulfa drugs, anti-malarial drugs, and anesthetics; in 1953 in antibiotics and insecticides, such as D.D.T. and 666.

The Chinese struggle against disease is no losing struggle. Far from it. Chinese health rapidly improves.

Medical science wins through and has many aids in its battle for positive health. Many factors help it. Economic advance with its higher standard of living, freedom of womanhood, lessened toil, advance of education and culture, the example of the People's Liberation Army, the teachability of the people bred of a new confidence in a Government which gives to the people immediate expression of its good will in food production, flood and drought control, and land distribution. All these factors and many more run hand in hand with deliberate attacks upon disease, and yield splendid and visible results.

The words of the International Scientific Commission neatly summarize China's health campaign:

"Since the Liberation there has been a health campaign in China of a breadth and scope probably hitherto unattained elsewhere. The wholehearted co-operation of every member of the population, man, woman, and child, has been necessary for the results which have been achieved. The clearing of accumulated rubbish, the scrupulous cleaning of courtyards and waste land, the screening of windows, the fight against all kinds of noxious insects, the production and use of insecticides and vaccines—every possible aspect of a constantly and rapidly rising general level of public health has been thought of and executed with verve and thoroughness. The fundamental education has been carried out by every available means of instruction, by large meetings, by posters, picture books and wall newspapers, by the press, from the stage and on the screen.

When confronted with bacteriological warfare the peasant masses of China knew what to do and did it without the least confusion or panic.

Only the support of the mass of the people of all classes could have achieved so much progress in so short a time.

If you want visible proof that the struggle is bearing fruit, go into the streets of any town or village of China. See the rising generation. See the boys and girls. See the babies as they lie in their mothers' arms or toddle bare to the skin on a hot summer's day along the city pavements or in the lanes. You need seek no further proof that health-conscious China is producing a vital, vigorous, and exuberantly happy race.

If you want to see the proof that the struggle is bearing fruit---See the rising generation.

2 All China Goes to School

THIRST for education goes hand in hand with social revolution. It was so in Russia. It was so in Spain. It is so in China. Education in China, as in Monarchial Spain, and as, earlier in tsarist Russia, had been for the well-to-do, not for common folk, however eagerly desired.

It is no more an accident today that you will see old folks in China struggling to master Chinese characters than it is to see in Scanteia, in the formerly education-starved Romania, the finest book-publishing establishment in the world, a grand expression of the thirst of a liberated people for the rich world opened up by education.

But an education to serve the masses in China faces formidable obstacles. A population twice as large as all Western Europe, 80 percent illiterate; an educational system designed to suit the needs of the ruling class in old China and content to leave 80 percent of Chinese citizens illiterate, with primary school accomodation for less than 40 percent of school-age children; an ancient and distinguished cultural past, highly civilized when the English people were woad-dyed savages, but a culture uncommunicated as yet to the Chinese working millions; an intellectual élite, from which teachers were chosen, steeped in American imperialist ideas. All that, and in addition a script complicated and hard to learn; a system ill equipped with books, buildings, and teachers and hampered by a long tradition that the intellectuals were the "clean" people, the manual workers the dirty people—and we begin to appreciate the obstacles which faced the progressive educationalists of the new China.

Simplification of Chinese script was a priority task. The difficult technique of reading in China has hitherto created an insuperable barrier against the development of a Chinese literary public. To read Chinese requires knowledge of some 1,000 or 1,500 separate characters.

With a new ingenious system of instruction, however, the door to reading has been opened somewhat wider; an intelligent man with this new technique—widely employed in the Red Army—can pick his way through a newspaper after three or four weeks' study.

Enthusiasm for mastery of reading knows no bounds. It is no uncommon sight to see the Chinese character for a gate pinned on to a gate, or for a cow stuck on the back of a cow, or a house on a house, a tree on a tree, so that the aspiring farmer and his wife may win familiarity with the form of the Chinese letter for the object, and experience the delight of recognizing it as they worry their way through the text of a Chinese newspaper. The new script is not yet taught in primary, junior, and middle schools. Its use or further development there is postponed to a later date.

Another primary obstacle has been the personnel of the teachers. Saturated with the ideas of the old China that education was for the élite and not the masses; saturated with ideas derived from American imperialistic aims and commercial ethics—many of China's teachers had their training in American schools and colleges, subtly endowed by the Boxer indemnity funds—the educational personnel needed a jolt.

The action of the U.S.A. in Taiwan, Korea, and Northern China, together with American blockade of Chinese waters and American boasts and warlike utterances, have provided the needed impetus to remold China's teachers and intellectuals. The cultural movement in China has become anti-exclusive, anti-imperialist, and anti-feudal, a culture belonging to, and operating for, the people.

This Chinese culture, the fountainhead from which China's education flows, as defined by Chairman Mao, is national, scientific, and popular: "It is opposed to the oppression of the imperialists, it maintains the dignity and independence of the Chinese nation; it is linked with the socialist and new democratic culture of other nations, establishing with them such relations as mutual absorption and mutual development so that each and all may become part of the culture of the new world."

These guiding principles are clearly embodied in the Common Program and have been written into its educational clauses. They define the general line of educational development of new China. An education for all children, to be realized as soon as teachers, together with buildings and equipment, are available. The future of the rising generation is guaranteed. Education is assured for that quarter of the human race which is situated in the Far Eastern world—a stupendous step forward in world culture.

Nor are the present multitudes of illiterates forgotten. Just as strenuous are the efforts made to bring culture to the adult masses as to provide full education for the rising generation.

Those who plan the new education in China are fully conscious of the difficulties ahead. But despite all, they are determined that within a dozen years or less all China shall enjoy a broad-based, balanced and rich educational culture, that manual work shall go hand in hand with intellectual work, that the manual worker, industrial or agricultural, shall read and write with ease, that literature appropriate to the new democratic character of the land shall stand ready to his hand in cheap abundance, that higher education shall be available for all, for women as well as men, for farmer as well as factory worker, for Tibetans and Mongolians and all minority peoples as well as for the Han Chinese. They are determined that education in its widest sense shall be open for all, regardless of sex, age, color, race, or creed.

They tackle the problem at both ends: small children at one end, adults at the other.

And that means that Chinese schools for some half-dozen years will be interim schools. First the ordinary primary school, compulsory and free for every child up to twelve years of age: a goal not yet attained but daily approached. Beyond that the junior middle school, up to fifteen years. Then comes the senior middle school, up to eighteen years of age.

Vocational middle schools, polytechnic, normal, medical schools, and schools for adults, with the same status as the regular schools.

Beyond eighteen are universities, institutes, or colleges, or alternatively a three-year course at a technicum.

Beyond those again are research institutes.

All adults can share in the educational system of China. Parallel with the curriculum for children, through primary, junior middle, and senior middle schools, or through the vocational middle schools alternative to these two latter—are spare-time primary, junior middle, and senior middle schools for adults, with the same status as the regular schools.

In this *interim* period, where education is both uniform in content and flexible in mode, there will be no age limits bounding the various forms of education. None will be barred from primary or middle school education, and from certificates for the same, because they lacked opportunity for schooling in the past.

Wide facilities are provided for adult education. Should regular school buildings be wanting for spare-time adult learners, then room must be made somewhere, anywhere: lessons are held in any suitable place—corners of workshops, dining rooms, dormitories.

More serious than shortage of school buildings is the shortage of trained teachers, met, as to the future, by providing higher education at the universities with living and tuition expenses paid for all who desire it and pass the qualifying examinations. For the immediate emergency there is streamlining and simplification of the curriculum used and special short courses of three years for teachers.

"It is hoped that in seven or ten years' time there will appear in China tens of thousands of highly educated intelligentsia from the workers and peasant classes, playing an indispensable role in China's economic, cul-

That the manual worker industrial and agricultural worker alike shall be able to read and write.

tural and national defense construction, together with intelligentsia from other social classes, likewise determined to serve the country, the people, the workers, the peasants and the soldiers." Here is the seed-ground from which new China's teachers will come.

The quality of the teachers is most important. The intellectual élite, still riddled with imperialistic, class or fascist ideas and unconscious of the fact, need re-education—"remolding" is the word used. That too it done. Done already by those who were the cream of the intellectual élite of China and are now making education available for all. The highly educated, highly cultured Mao Tse-tung, prime leader in the new education of China, puts it well in a statement quoted in Edgar Snow's *Red Star over China*:

"I will tell you my own experience in changing my feelings towards the people. When I was in school I picked up the habit of the students.

I felt awkward about doing any manual labor. For instance, I was embarrassed when I carried my own luggage on a bamboo pole in presence of students who could not bear the weight of anything across their shoulders and who could not carry anything in their hands. At that time I felt that the cleanest people in the world were the intellectuals. Workers, peasants and soldiers, they were always dirty people. . . .

"After the revolution I lived with workers, peasants and soldiers. Gradually I came to know them. They also began to know me. At this time, and only at this time, could I fundamentally change the feelings of the bourgeois and the petty-bourgeois that I had acquired in bourgeois schools. After this, in comparing unreformed intellectuals with workers, peasants and soldiers, I felt that such intellectuals had many unclean places, not only in their minds, but also in their bodies. The cleanest people in the world were the workers and the peasants . . . that is what I mean by a change of feeling—a change from one class to another."

That passage, extravagant perhaps to English bourgeois ears, strikes a major keynote of the character of the new, democratic education aimed at: it illuminates the problems of re-educating the present generation of teachers in order to free the minds of Chinese youth and adults from class, capitalist and imperialist taints.

Education proceeds by leaps and bounds. Peasants who, ignorant of their real contents, signed with their fingerprints documents which mortgaged away their farms, mothers who signed documents which sold their daughters to a brothel and not, as they were told, admitted them to a factory, are naturally eager to read that they may understand the documents they sign. Farmers are eager to read of agriculture, mechanics of machines. The Chinese masses suddenly see an open road to learning.

Here are the figures of students during 1952, compared with the highest figures under the Kuomintang: Students in institutes of higher learning, 218,000, or 169.9 percent increase; students in middle schools, 3,070,000, or 163.9 percent increase; primary school pupils, 49,000,000, or 207 percent increase.

Here and in the drive for adult education is justification for the title of this chapter—All China Goes to School.

3 New Cultural Horizons

CHINESE literary culture, like Chinese science, passes through its stages of re-education, remaking, rebirth. Facts enforced the change. New steps in education, giving birth to a new working class proletarian intelligentsia, lead inevitably to new demands upon literature. As the masses begin to read, they seek literature which deals with things of today, things which interest them; things which enlighten, stimulate, and encourage them in their tasks. A new literature simple in form and using simplified script.

This presented a serious problem for cultured Chinese writers; demanding a descent from the rarefied air of Chinese literature, with its banal themes but charming turn of phrase. It might seem too hard for a man with delicate literary taste like Lao Sheh to work in this circumscribed medium. Not so, however, when he was writing for the workers, the revolution, and the reconstruction of Chinese life. For though a man with the ancient Chinese culture at his finger-tips—he is indeed head of the imperial Manchu family—his heart and soul are in the Liberation Movement. He loves the people and will work himself to the bone for them. Indeed, he does so, for he is delicate. We saw him in his own home.

Lao Sheh is a charming host and lives in a charming and typically upper class Peking house which, once seen, is never forgotten.

Approached by a narrow alley-way, unpaved as a country lane, though in the heart of Peking, barely wide enough to admit a modern car and too small for two to pass, bounded by high, windowless walls, punctuated with massive doors opening inward and onto a charming courtyard, severed from too abrupt entrance by large solid movable screens. From this outer courtyard, with its flowering trees and goldfish tubs, one enters a second courtyard, still more gay with flowers and flowering shrubs.

On either side and in front are low rooms, capable of opening almost along their whole length. The buildings here and indeed all over Peking are only one room high and overtopped by trees, giving the city a calm and country-like serenity. These Peking courtyards, silent, airy, bright, and sunny, entirely shut off from the city world, open only but wholly to the heavens, are the last word in civic architectural culture.

And Lao Sheh's room, with its low Chinese tables of black wood, its lovely old carved, backless barrel-shaped stools, on one of which Lao Sheh himself sat as we talked, matched the home. The walls were hung with painted scrolls of great beauty, some old and some the work of a living painter, ninety-three-year old Chi Pai-shih.

In this typical home of the Peking upper class—similar, doubtless, to Peking homes 500 years ago—Lao Sheh, one with the new China's common people, fighting with them in peril during the long, upward struggle against the Kuomintang tyranny, now writes for them in their own script, to meet and aid them in their out-reach for a fuller life.

In this same room we met Madame Tin Ling, China's leading woman novelist. Together they spoke of the new problems presented to Chinese writers by the new life and the new simplified script. The masses demand literature which reflects their life and struggle, but they demand it in so simple a script that they themselves can read it. That first; and then the stories must be short, reflecting and inspiring the peasant struggles and triumphs and quickly produced: the hunger for books brooks no delay.

Both authors emphasized the great difficulty for writers like themselves, brought up in the old school with its love of leisurely writing and sensitive feeling for form and rich language. Both writers spoke modestly of their new achievements. Lao Sheh spoke as if he must retire from the literary struggle. Yet no man in China has won his way more thoroughly to the heart of the people or been a greater force for the new construction work than Lao Sheh himself, with his play, *The Dragon Beard Ditch,* and no woman in China has won her way to the heart of the people more thoroughly than Madame Ting with her *Sunshine over the Sangan River.*

This Chinese renaissance is not precisely new, though the Liberation has given it new life. It began on May 4, 1919, when British and American plans to give Shantung to the Japanese struck a spark which set all China ablaze. Acting under popular pressure the Chinese Government refused to ratify the treaty, students and intellectuals awakening with a start to realities began to study the new Soviet Union and the literature which inspired it. Marx and Lenin, in translation, took their place beside Confucius and Mencius.

This new intellectual revolt found its natural home at the headquarters of the new Red Army, whose leader, Mao Tse-tung, found time in May, 1942, despite bitter and critical warfare, to discuss with writers and artists at Yenan their work and contribution to the revolution—proof incidentally of Mao's confidence in the sequel of the struggle.

Mao's summing up of the conference has since been published in book form under the title *Problems of Art and Literature,* a book I enjoyed on the Canton-Peking express, with the thermometer standing at over 100 degrees. It is remarkable piece of work, and its ideas will exercise a profound influence on all Chinese art and literature.

Mao's basic theme is that it is the people who must provide the inspiration for the artist and their activities the material for his work. Ninety percent of China's millions are workers, peasants, soldiers, or small middle-class craftsmen and merchants. From these millions and the profound emotions that move them China's artists must take their themes. To these millions they must present their works for criticism or use. These millions are the people who do things, make things, use things. They are the people who matter. They are the living, growing edge of Chinese humanity. Deep are the mines of wealth among the common people. Get among them, says Mao, think with them, work with them, struggle with them. Write about their problems, their aims and aspirations, especially in this moment of their new life. And write in the language and with the images that they can understand.

A mighty movement has gripped the people. New horizons appear. Grasp and share the big hopes that inspire the people as they see their fellow men and fellow women liberated.

The people will judge whether you aid or hinder them. The people will be your audience. Write simply and directly, but in the best style at your command. Nothing but the best in form can match the best in content. Mao Tse-tung puts it in a sentence when he condemns "artistic products with reactionary content and creations with merely the style of placards and slogans which have only content and no form."

Under Mao's inspiration, Chinese artists and writers left their dens of "escapism." They went into field, factory, and army, went and lived, and wrote as they lived. The little poems of slender content but exquisite form no longer issue from the pens of China's leading writers. Themselves in the full flood of China's struggles and achievements, their writings reflect the deep emotions which they share with the people.

So great indeed was the thrill of living through these days that men and women who never had written a word before, who could neither read nor write, were consumed with an urge to express what they were feeling, and use that expression to heighten the fires in neighboring lives. China began to produce her own writers, springing straight from the struggling masses, writing about themselves and their comrades in building socialism, defending their liberties from external attack or internal deviation, themselves in heroic deeds and great constructions.

Exceptionally remarkable, for example, is the literary achievement of Kao Pao, China's soldier-writer. Born into a poor peasant family, he passed his childhood in inconceivable poverty and bitter humiliation under Japanese domination and the vicious rule of Chinese puppets and landlords. His landlord owner had rejected the offer of a teacher to give this bright child a free education. Bitterly grieved, Kao grew up without schooling. At the age of eight he became a swineherd.

Famine drove him to Dairen, where he found employment as a laborer. Every evening the young lad sat spellbound, listening to professional story-tellers recounting chivalrous deeds of ancient heroes. Wounded by a dynamite blast on railway work, Kao borrowed a simple book to study while he convalesced. He only knew 200 characters, but friends helped him to learn more and he struggled through.

In 1947 he joined the Liberation Army, became a Party member, was commended on eight separate occasions and won the title of "Meritorious People's Servant."

Soaked in heroic classic material, he became an inspiring story-teller to his soldier comrades. Slowly, in the meantime, he mastered more characters through attending the Army literacy classes.

During those years Kao marched across the whole length of China, south to north, sharing to the full hardship and struggle. At Changsha, in August, 1949, he came across this striking sentence in a pictorial narrative called *Mao Tse-tung's Boyhood*: "Why is it that the principal characters of all the stories I have read are either generals or talented young men and beautiful ladies? Why are they never people like honest peasants?"

The very next day, in a new booklet distributed to the Army, he read of a hero who was a poor man. The story reminded Kao of the wrongs he had suffered, of his grandfather, mother, uncle, and brother, all hounded to early graves; of people tortured by Japanese imperialists and their puppets. He decided to write a book of his own life.

After writing for two days, Kao found that he knew only 25 percent of the words or ideographs needed to express his thoughts. Sorely tempted to give up, he kept repeating to himself Lenin's words: "Study, study and study again." Determined to go on, he made temporary symbols of his own to represent the characters he could not write.

We wrote with passion, to fortify others to maintain the struggle against the enemies of the people. "If I can't finish the book in one year, I'll work on it for two. If two years aren't enough, let it be five."

His army senior learned of his effort and encouraged him by appointing a comrade to assist him. He worked hard, sweating with concentration and never resting at night until he had finished the section on which he was working. Even on the march he wrote. When hungry and exhausted he wrote.

At first he wrote in verse. Advised by older comrades, he rewrote the whole of the first ten chapters in prose.

When the Korean War broke out he wrote more fiercely still. He worked on until two or even three in the morning. At last in January, 1951, his autobiographical novel of more than sixty chapters, *Kao Yu-pao,* was completed, and has had a wide circulation. The editors of the *People's Army Literature Magazine,* greatly struck with its living, literary character, had already published the first three chapters in full as a sample of the work.

Kao's novel is a vital piece of work struck off in the heat of the struggle, crystallizing an important period and issuing from the pen of a boy of genius inspired by New China's most creative movement.

Every aid is given to would-be authors. The Central Literary Institute, directed by Madame Ting Ling, provides a two-year course, with study, board, and lodging free. Ku Mo-jo, Lao Sheh, and other famous writers give lectures to the students. Its fifty-one members are of worker-peasant background; the great majority were revolutionary workers in the Anti-Japanese War.

Nor is it only writers who express the new Chinese culture.

China's cultural life expands in all directions, new writing, new painting, new theater, new cinema.

If there is any redeeming feature to the appalling rift which now separates East from West, it lies in the fact that China's cinemas start with a clean sheet. Hollywood productions neither enter China now nor are sought there. The huge market which once was open to U.S. films is now closed and likely to remain so until Hollywood is purged from its crudity, its brutality, and its low sexual morality. The cinema-going public of China feed on nobler fare. To return from Russia, Eastern Europe, or China to the "Christian West" never fails to yield its shock as one sees advertisements of Western films on Western hoardings. Films in the Eastern world are clean and serious, and film advertisements are clean and reflect a serious and cleanly life—a standard not yet reached in the West.

The life of Chinese men and women is too full of creative activity to seek "escape" in fatuous or horrific films; the youth, full of adventure

and, enabled if they wish it, to embark on early and satisfying married life, do not seek the stimulation of coarse sexual films. During the past three years China has produced eighty-six feature films, fifty-seven documentary films and imported 101 films from the Soviet Union with Chinese dialogue. The Chinese film industry has been afforded a splendid new start and has taken it.

Reformed Chinese opera advances side by side with the reformed Chinese cinema. Opera has been in vogue in China for many centuries. Before the Liberation it was purely formal in character and planned in content to cultivate qualities suitable to feudal life.

Differing widely from Western forms, China's opera was gorgeous in robes, bereft of scenery, and full of complicated symbolism bewildering to a Westerner. Singing in Chinese opera was artificial and bound to remain so as long as men took the women's parts and developed a painful falsetto.

The themes of the old opera were constant—humility, patience, submission to despots, filial piety, and abject womanly obedience.

But opera, like all Chinese life, has changed. Music has changed. China has learned much in mode and orchestration from the West. Folk-tunes collected from the countryside and from the national minorities form a treasure house for the solos, orchestration, or choruses required by composers.

The White-Haired Girl, with its thrills of liberation, or *The Dragon Beard Ditch,* with its thrill of the new cleanliness achieved by collective effort replacing the old and the foul, give a vivid hint of the themes of the new Chinese opera.

And not least is the change in the life lived by the men and now women performers. No longer are professional actors—and they number above 200,000—dancers or musicians considered more menial than servants and pushed down to the level of "untouchables." No longer is the boy apprentice condemned to daily beatings and years of work without pay, followed subsequently by huge deductions by agents from his earnings. Actors and actresses can now learn their art free of charge and in honorable conditions at special institutes. Chinese actors today are regarded as men worthy of all honor, serving a noble profession vitally useful to the people.

Chinese culture plunges headlong into its renaissance.

4 Science Comes to the People

PRE-REVOLUTIONARY culture in China was not of and for the people. Neither was Chinese science of and for the people. Chinese culture spread itself out for the élite, for the select few. It was esoteric. Chinese science also was esoteric. It was exclusive, a closed order.

Stemming largely from Western science, Chinese science was individualistic to a marked degree. The quest for abstract truth was its sole purpose. To select a subject in his own field, study it intensively, regardless of the needs of the people for investigation in a thousand directions, led each scientist to do exactly as he liked.

Pre-liberation scientists never realized that in the last resort they owed their livelihood and the funds to carry on their researches to the working people. Nor did they realize the importance of creating a scientifically-minded public, which was precisely the aim of the Liberation Government.

A "science-conscious" people was the goal: "Scientific knowledge shall be disseminated among the people," says the People's Common Program.

Not an easy task by any means, for not only were scientists content to live and work in isolation, unmoved by the people and their needs, but also the people themselves in their profound ignorance knew nothing about science and cared less. Passing his miserable life in toil and poverty, the peasant—and 80 percent of the people were peasants—was content with the rule of thumb inherited from his ancestors. If he were poor and the landlord rich, that was fate.

Crippling superstitions which rule sowing and reaping, not by the weather or by reason but by priestly decisions and religious festivals, always and in every country depart as science dawns.

That dawn was heralded for the peasant farmer of China in a way he could understand, by means of the farm tools which the People's Government provided.

An engineer, Li Tsung-ke, took one of the new plows to a farm in Hopei Province. He described his reception:

"We saw a peasant plowing beside the highway. The village government worker who accompanied me asked the man to unhitch the old wooden plow and try the new one. He plowed to the end of his field and back and exclaimed: 'This is really something! See how deep and wide the furrows are. And it is so light, the mule no longer gets tired.' And when he took his hands off the plough it neither lurched nor lay on its side like the old one. Fearful of losing this wonderful new tool, he exclaimed: 'Don't take it away. Sell it to me now. A child could run it.' An old man standing by exclaimed when he saw it tear up a piece of waste land tangled with stubborn grass roots: 'If I had possessed that plow before, this piece of land would not have been wasted for the past three years.'"

Early in 1950, at three cultural centers, popular science exhibitions were enthusiastically welcomed by the peasants. The new implements proved the great draw. The crush to see the new plow was so great that it was moved out of the building into the open. What each peasant sought was the immediate means for increased production. They got what they sought and more too, for the thin end of the wedge had penetrated. The young men and women sought further knowledge. Science centers and museums were founded, lectures were arranged. Science talks on the radio, science columns in newspapers—in forty-one of them, including the Peking *People's Daily*—realized the demand and met it.

Factory workers as well as agricultural laborers sought advanced scientific and technical knowledge to improve their tools and extend the range of tool operation. This initial quest, stimulated and broadened out by exhibitions and lectures on physiology and hygienics, or on modes of coping with various diseases, enlarged the range of popular scientific understanding. Coal enterprises sought technicians to increase efficiency and secure health in working. Lectures on tissue serum therapy and vernalization of grains commanded wide audiences.

The ill-planned, poorly attended, old-fashioned scientific institutions, too self-centered, too sectarian, had utterly failed. They needed a radical overhaul and received it.

Chinese scientists are at last shaking themselves free from the old strangling tendency of detachment from the practical applications of science, with exclusive devotion to theoretical speculation. Scientific institutions cease to provide a hideout for men who find social and political conditions intolerable. They become workshops to aid people who strive to move to fullness of living.

Scientific research in the new China bends itself eagerly to meet the needs of agriculture, industry and public health. Co-ordinated under the

Chinese Academy of Science, with Ku Mo-jo, the world scholar and winner of the Stalin Peace Prize, at its head, research work in China addresses itself to the needs of society, tackles the vital problems facing the people, at the same time training scientific workers in preparation for the construction of a modern industrial China. "The science of the future," in the words of Professor Bernal, "must be socially planned."

Take, in illustration of the new work, the experimental station at Tsingtao, focused on the study of marine life; or another station on Taiho Lake to study the nature and habits of fresh-water fish; or, again, the Institute of Systematic Botany in Peking, with its emphasis upon the study of economic plants—medicinal herbs, pasture grasses, or plants providing rubber latex.

An interesting example of science harnessed for the benefit of farms and factories, thus linking theory and practice, a fundamental Communist principle, occurs in the important cotton-producing areas of Hopei, Honan Province, where 1.5 million acres of cotton lands have been heavily infested with the cotton aphis, which has reduced the crop by about one-third. Entomologists have hitherto assumed that this aphis lived on some "host" plant above the ground throughout the year and must there be sought and attacked. Dr. Chu Hung-fu shows that this is not so. The aphis hibernates in the soil, and there and from thence must be attacked, a conclusion which has led to most valuable results.

Reorganization of the old institutions was urgently needed, and amalgamation of institutions has been one effectual way of reorganization. For instance, the Institute of Meteorology has been enlarged into an Institute of Geophysics and Meteorology and includes departments of geographical survey and seismological research. Close co-operation has been secured between the meteorological department of the Institute and the Government Weather Bureau. Thus the scientist has one foot on earth, if the other foot is in the clouds; he helps, and learns by helping, his fellow men to understand earthquakes and weather and where to dig to secure new rich materials for the people's industry.

Furthermore, these institutions are widely spread in various parts of the country and to some of them are attached experimental stations, observatories and other research establishments, such as aquariums and botanical gardens.

Research in the stricter sense is by no means neglected despite concentration on practical affairs. Research runs along side by side with the solution of current problems. Various kinds of raw materials are collected and tested with a view to their fullest utilization—latex-yielding plants, for instance, and preparations of insecticides and fungicides out of organo-mercuric compounds, together with various kinds of herbs of therapeutical value long known to Chinese medicine.

The study of parasites in fresh-water fish in the Yangtze Estuary has facilitated improved production in the fresh-water fishing industry. For use as an experimental station of genetics and plant-breeding, a large area is devoted to testing out traditional methods used by peasants in North China to treat the seeds of their crops and check the results with those obtained by Michurin methods.

The locating and evaluating of the mineral deposits of China and detailed surveys of the physico-topographic conditions of key areas required by railway construction and river conservation loom large: eighty-three parties were already at work in 1951 in geological and paleontological explorations.

Scientific workers in every case are encouraged to adopt collective methods of research, to work in teams, to shake themselves free from a perverted sense of possession, even of ideas. Individualism in science, as elsewhere, must be replaced by collectivism. Emphasis concentrates always and everywhere on instruments to create, not on instruments to destroy. Helping, not dominating, fellow men is the keynote of peace-loving Chinese science.

5 Landmarks of the Christian Church in China

RELIGION can serve the deepest needs of honest men. Bent and twisted, it can serve the purpose of unscrupulous men. Never more so than now. Many bitter opponents of the Liberation and Socialist movements in China, who have small use for the ethics of the Christian religion at home, and oppose it ruthlessly when it thwarts their interests, vehemently allege, through controlled press, radio, and cinema, that Christians are suffering grievous persecution in Russia, Eastern Europe, and China. Knowing that the British and American public hold religion in respect and can readily be enlisted against persecutors of Christians, they raise the cry, "Religion is at stake," adding the corollary: "Arm to resist." It is a trump card.

As in Russia and Eastern Europe, where I had tested the charges on the spot and after talking to Church leaders in each country had found them groundless, so too in China I sought to learn on the spot the realities of the religious situation. My travels took me north, south, east, and west—to Peking, Hankow, Changsha, Canton, Hangchow, Shanghai, Nanking, Pengpu, Tientsin, and Mukden, where I sought contact wherever time permitted, with leaders of the several Christian churches, Episcopal, Congregational, Methodist, Baptist, Presbyterian, Roman Catholic, and with the Y.M.C.A., Y.W.C.A. and other Christian bodies.

I preached in the Anglican—now renamed the Holy Catholic—Church in Shanghai with three Chinese bishops present; in the Methodist Church in Peking, and in the Baptist Church in Canton, as being the biggest buildings for the crowded congregations.

I had long conferences with Christian leaders in all great centers, including Roman Catholics, starting with a three-hour session in Peking, under the chairmanship of the Rev. T. C. Wong, Congregational Minister and General Secretary of the North China Christian Federation. Eighteen directors and leaders in the field of religion in the Protestant churches were present, including Bishop T. H. Y. Lin, Methodist ministers and leaders of the Y.M.C.A., Y.W.C.A., and Salvation Army.

All spoke freely and frankly, often with quiet passion. This, and other similar conferences, left me with the general impression of a vigorous forward-looking body of Christian leaders, welcoming a social life much nearer to that they preached than anything formerly experienced. In the words spoken to me later in Shanghai by the elderly Bishop T. Lindel Tsen, whom I had last met in Canterbury in 1948: "It is easier now to speak openly against vice, against dishonesty or the like, than under the Kuomintang. Now I can preach my mind happily."

The Christian Church in China, it was explained, needed, and had received, a surgical operation. Of this they spoke honestly. The full implications were explained to me in detail later by Dr. V. T. Wu, for thirty years Executive Secretary of the Literature Division of the National Y.M.C.A. of China, a graduate of Columbia University and the Union Theological Seminary in the U.S.A., and one of the Christian leaders who started in July, 1950, the flourishing Christian Reform Movement which has assumed the leadership of the Christian churches in China. He now serves as Chairman of its Committee.

Dr. Wu outlined the links between Christianity in China and Western imperialism—often unconscious, but none the less real links—since the introduction of Protestant Christianity in 1807. The first missionary, an Englishman, Robert Morrison, was concurrently a vice-consul and employee of the East India Company. Letters home from the first American missionary, E. C. Bridgman, spoke of the importance of the political aspect of missionary work. In 1844 Bridgman and two of his co-workers, Peter Parker and S. Wells William, were instrumental in forcing on China the Wanghsia (Cushing) Treaty which gave the U.S. extra-territorial and other privileges. In 1857 Peter Parker made a proposal to the State Department for the annexation of Taiwan (Formosa).

American missionary writings—here they differ widely from British missionary writings—openly regarded the missionary movement as the cultural spearhead for political and military invasion. Arthur H. Smith, who worked as a missionary for thirty years in China, approvingly quotes in his book, *China and America Today,* from a memorandum sent to the President of the United States in 1906 by Edmund J. James, President of the University of Illinois: "The nation which succeeds in educating the young Chinese of the present generation will be the nation which for a given expenditure of effort will reap the largest possible returns in moral, intellectual and commercial influence. . . . Trade follows moral and spiritual domination far more uncritically than it follows the flag."

In China, in consequence, there were thirteen Christian universities supported by American funds, 203 hospitals, 320 orphanages, 15,000 Christian university graduates, and 250,000 students in Christian schools.

Through a century and a half the connection has been maintained, and contemporary American missionary writings often quite openly regard the missionary movements as the cultural spearhead for political and economic invasion. The ordinary American missionary workers were quite honest, Dr. Wu asserts. He describes their attitude as follows:

"American civilization and the American way of life are the best in the world. They are mainly, if not totally, Christian, and must be pressed and spread at all costs—to China and the world. Any threat to the priceless possession of the American people is an enemy not only of the American people, but of the whole world, including Christianity. It must be wiped out wherever it appears, by peaceful means if possible, but by war if necessary. It is the missionary's holy mission to accomplish this task."

Rewi Alley, in his excellent book, *Yo Banfa!* gives several instances corroborating Dr. Wu's statement. Here is one:

"I remember one hot summer's night when the guests, fanning themselves, sat around the feet of an elderly American bishop, seeking the episcopal guidance on a number of troublesome problems. . . .

"The bishop, an old China hand, firmly brought all wavering elements together and gave directions in no uncertain manner: 'The best and in the last analysis, the only thing that can happen to China is to incorporate it into the United States of America, on a state basis. We shall send the administrators, the technicians . . . it has been shown that the only people who can really get things done in China are the foreigners, and of the foreigners the Americans only will have the virility, the cultural and industrial potential great enough to lead. The docile, hard-working peasants of China will welcome them. . . .'"

In this respect Alley sees small difference between Catholic and Protestant missionaries. He records how the Belgian Catholic mission at Saratsi —I stayed a night there with Major Todd in 1932—was a power in the land, firmly in control of a great many people, with arms stored away under their churches. . . . The Catholic Church in many places was rich: it grew rich by taking over lands in times of drought for the price of a little food.

On the other hand, the last American Ambassadar to China was one of the oldest China Coast Protestant missionaries, Leighton Stuart. Or, yet again, there was the tall, Prussian Catholic father in Alley's own city of Sandan, "who hovered about looking for information and taking it along to the Kuomintang *hsien* government, and found it convenient to vanish some time before liberation and turn up again in the Philippines."

Imbued with these imperialistic and Western ideas, Dr. Wu proceeds, the missionary fitted into the imperialist scheme of aggression. He lived in a garden compound with modern facilities. He was in fact, if not in name, boss of his Church and Christian organization because he controlled its finances, which came from abroad, together with its policies. I would merely add to this here, as I did in China itself, that in my experience it is decidedly less true of English missionaries, whose houses and lives are simpler and whose teaching is more evangelistic with a tendency to other-worldliness: I never saw a grand piano and evening dress in a British missionary's Chinese home. I saw both at an American mission.

The surgical operation which Chinese Christianity needed was decisive severance once and for all of the Chinese Church from the imperialists of the West. The Chinese Church must stand, as many British missionaries, my own missionary kinfolk among them, had long urged, upon its own feet, financially and in its organization.

This operation brought Christian missions from the West to an abrupt end. It severed at one stroke century-old ties. It was a drastic operation, but the Chinese Church has met it and survived. Has indeed, I believe, profited by it. The Church itself receives new respect from many Chinese patriots who were formerly suspicious of its imperialist origins and connections.

The rural churches have suffered most: 80 percent have failed to survive as organized bodies. The rural churches, working amid poverty-stricken peasants, with a minimum of middle class traders and merchants, were dependent to a much larger extent than the city churches upon foreign aid.

The attitude of the Government to the Church has been not unfriendly. Many in the Government, as elsewhere, doubtless think that religion is obsolete. Certainly religion never made its voice heard in emphatic protest against the glaring abuses and anti-social acts of the Kuomintang, the feudal landlords, or the imperialist aggressors. Despite all that, the Government's attitude has been conciliatory.

This was shown markedly when Chou En-lai, the Premier, together with several other high officials, and at a time when he was overwhelmed with pressing Government business, personally attended the conference in which the Church had sought to meet officials of the Central People's Government. The Premier informed the delegates that he was glad to have the opportunity of discussing Church affairs with them.

Chou En-lai then went straight to the root of the matter. He stated that the difficulties of the Church, from a State point of view, sprang from fears of the entanglement of Church officials and Church people generally with imperialism. The Church could indeed only solve its problem by complete dissociation from every imperialist connection abroad, rooting out also all imperialistic elements in its own life. Christians, he added, must beware of "being used." Defining imperialism as the use by one country of money or force to impose its own culture or trade upon another country, so that it virtually became a colony or a semi-colony of the aggressive power, he urged the Church to make its severance with imperialism complete and final. The Church must become independent—self-governing, self-supporting, self-propagating. It must, he also added, give up its non-political attitude, for politics were inseparable from the responsibilities of good citizenship.

Here was the challenge to Christian leaders. Here was their opportunity for playing their own distinctive part in China's reconstruction. Here was indeed a landmark in the history of the Church in China.

Out of this situation grew the Chinese Reform Movement, begun on July 28, 1950, when forty Chinese Christian leaders issued a statement on the task of Christianity in the new China. This was endorsed almost immediately by 1,527 Christian leaders of various denominations, who called on their fellow Christians:

1. To support China's new basic law, the Common Program.
2. To liquidate imperialist influence within the Church and guard against plots to use Christianity for reactionary purposes.
3. To end reliance upon foreign personnel and finance and build up a self-supporting, and self-propagating Chinese Church.

A manifesto endorsing these demands was issued, entitled *The Task of the Chinese Christian Movement in National Reconstruction in New China.* It opens with these words:

"Protestant Christianity has been introduced to China for more than one hundred and forty years. During this period it has made a not unworthy contribution to Chinese society. Nevertheless, and this was most unfortunate, not long after Christianity's coming to China, imperialism started its activities here; and since the principal groups of missionaries who brought Christianity to China all came from these imperialist countries, Christianity consciously or unconsciously, directly or indirectly, became related with imperialism. Now that the Chinese revolution has achieved victory, these imperialist countries will not rest passively content in face of this unprecedented historical fact in China. They will certainly seek to contrive by every means the destruction of what has actually been achieved; they may also make use of Christianity to forward their plot of stirring up internal dissension and creating reactionary forces in this country. It is our purpose in publishing the following Statement to heighten our vigilance against imperialism, to make known the clear political stand of Christians in New China, to hasten the building of a Chinese Church whose affairs are managed by the Chinese themselves, and to indicate the responsibilities which should be taken up by Christians throughout the whole country in national reconstruction in New China. We desire to call upon all Christians in the country to exert their best efforts in putting into effect the principles herein presented."

The section entitled "The Task in General" says: "Christian Churches and organizations in China give thoroughgoing support to the 'Common Political Platform' and under the leadership of the Government oppose imperialism, feudalism, and bureaucratic capitalism, and take part in the effort to build an independent, democratic, peaceful, unified, prosperous, and powerful New China."

The section, "Concrete Methods," declares: "All Christian Churches and organizations in China which are still relying upon foreign personnel and financial aid should work out concrete plans to realize within the shortest possible time their objective of self-reliance and rejuvenation."

Dr. Wu tell me that he, like Professor Fletcher in America, Mr. Kenneth Ingram in England, Dr. Endicott in Canada, Bishop Mersoyan of the Moravian Church, and various clergy in Czechoslovakia, are seeking some of the deeper connections and possible intellectual bridges between Christianity and Communism. The following passage by a noted Chinese evangelist is significant, and shows that he is not alone in his quest:

"The Lord Jesus in whom we believe is He who opposed the imperialism of Rome, struck at the feudalism of Herod, and struggled against the bureaucratic capitalism of the High Priests and the Pharisees and was also by these three enemies nailed to His cross. The Lord Jesus once publicly proclaimed as His program of individual and social salvation: 'to preach good tidings to the poor, to proclaim release to the captives and recovering of sight to the blind, to set at liberty them that are bruised.' Furthermore, in my recent extensive reading of the books of Marx, Engels, Lenin, and Stalin, together with the thinking of Mao Tse-tung—and in particular in the *Capital* of Karl Marx—I have discovered that a great number of their arguments and theories are compatible with the teachings and doctrines of Jesus, and after reading them my faith in Christ and in the Bible has become stronger than ever."

The invasion of Korea, the freezing of Chinese assets, and now supremely the germ warfare have severed the last links with imperialism. The Chinese Christian Church stands at last on its own feet, and by that very fact, as was pointed out to me and as I have suggested earlier, has removed a barrier which had alienated it from much public sympathy.

A national Christian Council, unattended by any foreign missionary or minister, marks another milestone in Chinese Church life. This is the first all-Chinese Council ever held. It celebrated the coming of age of the Chinese Church.

These were the facts and this was the testimony I learned in Peking and elsewhere when I met the Chinese Church groups.

Bishop T. Lindel Tsen, for instance, the doyen of Anglican Chinese bishops, whom I entertained at tea in Canterbury in 1948, when with other bishops of the Anglican Church he had come to England for the Lambeth Conference, kindly put into the following paragraphs some of the relevant points of a long conversation we had together:

"As to the question of religious freedom, it is clearly and definitely stated in our Common Program that the people have full freedom in religious faith. Under this same principle the Christian Churches have organized a national committee for the Reformation of the Church in the matter of self-support, self-government, and self-propagation. . . . The Diocese of Honan, two weeks ago, consecrated an assistant bishop to meet the needs of the growing Church in that diocese. . . . Recently there were new ordinations in the dioceses of Hankow, Honan, and Nanking, sure signs of Church progress."

From many other sources could I quote similar testimony, but let this letter frôm another member of what was formerly an English Episcopal Mission, suffice for the moment. Bishop Michael Chang writes to me:

"Fukien can claim to have more churches and Christians than almost any other part of China, and it goes without saying that the Christians in Fukien have likewise been more permeated with the evil influence of capitalism and imperialism throughout the hundred years of our history. Therefore we are in the midst of a great effort to eradicate all these influences and to build up a Church belonging to the people of China and working for their true welfare, a Church which is self-governing, self-propagating. . . . All the seven bodies of Christians in Foochow have joined this organization and we are all now working together."

These two letters strike the leading notes of the present situation.

First, they emphasize the fact of past imperialist and capitalist pressure, conscious or unconscious, upon China through Christian missionaries, with the deliberate and determined effort to end it.

Second, they emphasize the fact of present religious freedom for the worship and the propaganda of Christianity.

Third, they emphasize the vitality and growth of the new Independent Christian Church in China.

Some further points, however, need explanation or emphasis.

First, though no persecution of missonaries or Christians has been countenanced by the Government, there may have been persecutions in isolated places. China is a vast land populated by people of many types. Much depends upon the past conduct of the Christian missions and missionaries as to the treatment they received at the moment of liberation. Had they been actively supporting the bitter persecution of Chiang Kai-shek in his opposition to the Liberation Movement? Had they taken no active part in seeking to restrain the brutalities of the feudal landlords, or protested against the shameful poverty of the peasant workers? Had they acted as informers or spies for imperialist powers?

Curiously enough, two of the missionaries with whom I had traveled in 1932 came under the latter category. One became an informer attached to the Chungking Government, the other turned up to see my friend Rewi Alley, at the time of the crisis, in the uniform of an American major, his son as a colonel, and driving a jeep loaded with weapons and ammunition. Naturally, there could be no friendly feelings by the non-Christian citizens toward these men, though I never heard that either of them was molested.

Secondly, education and health and educational and medical institutions have been placed under the sole control of the Government. China in this respect has followed much Western precedent. The extent of free treatment given would in any event have been beyond the financial possibilities of private hospitals. And foreign support had been entirely cut off. Yet no hospital could shut its doors. I visited one hospital, formerly an American medical mission station. The number of patients and staff was much increased and the pleasant modern residence of the missionary was being used for a variety of official purposes. The Chinese medical missions had started an excellent work. The Government, awakening to its responsibility and under the inspiration of the new health regime, is now indefinitely extending it. The same may be said of education.

The liquidation of imperialist influence within the Chinese Church became for a while the Church's major preoccupation. Only slowly did the facts come to light. At a large rally of 12,000 Christian people at Shanghai in June, 1951, the speakers gave accounts of their experiences with foreign missionaries. Accusations were made against a long list of people, foremost of whom was Frank W. Price, trusted American adviser to Chiang Kai-shek, who used the Chinese Church and its activities in the rural districts to uphold the Kuomintang regime and provide information to the American Government. The common charge alleged against a long list of foreign religious workers was that they had used Christianity as a tool to promote the interests of American imperialism.

This rally in Shanghai touched off similar meetings elsewhere, opening the eyes of many Christians to things they had neither known nor realized before. "It was not easy," writes Dr. Wu, "for a Chinese Christian to accuse another person, especially if the latter professed to be a Christian. 'Judge not that ye be not judged' is a teaching of Jesus which every Chinese Christian has learned. But," he adds, "they also know that Jesus Himself had accused the Scribes and Pharisees in the strongest terms. Awakened Christians now realize that accusation is merely a condemnation of evil in harmony with Christian teaching. They are fully conscious of the need of a house-cleaning in the Churches and Christian organizations of China."

One more word must be said before I come finally to speak of a supremely important contribution of the New Chinese Christian Church to their country. Rank-and-file Chinese Christians welcome the changes introduced by the Liberation Government without experiencing the pressure and anxieties which have exercised the leaders. Life for them in general is easier since the Liberation. Christian life especially is easier in a country which has experienced profound moral changes. It is easier to be an honest man when all around you are striving to be honest; easier to be humane when others beside you practice humanity; easier to be self-critical when self-criticism has become an accepted principle for many comrades and companions.

And now and lastly I come to the great contribution of the Chinese Church to world peace.

Supremely effective in severing the Christian Church in China from its entanglement with capitalist and imperialist America is the new germ warfare launched by the U.S.A., first against Korea and then against northeast China itself.

It is precisely here that the Christian Churches in China are able to strike their most vigorous blow for peace.

For the British public and the British Church leaders gave no credence to the charge of germ warfare against the U.S.A. when I left England late in May, 1952: "Merely Communist propaganda; it is impossible that the U.S.A. could entertain so monstrous an idea," was the attitude of religious people to the charge.

Realizing the importance of a declaration by the united body of Christian leaders in China on the matter, I made deliberate investigation in each major town throughout my journey as to the attitude of the local Church leaders toward the question of germ warfare, beginning at Peking and ending in Mukden, the focal center of germ attack in northeast China.

I returned to England with highly important documents presented with great formality entirely on their own initiative by the Christians in China to the Christians in England, challenging them to join the Chinese Christian Churches in denouncing an act of wickedness never equaled before. On the plea of defending "Christian civilization," it is urged, an effort has been made to scatter exterminating disease on the masses of Chinese. "The Christian civilization," they ironically add, which sent medical missions to China, able at best to save but a small fragment of China's millions from disease, now threatens to liquidate many more through disease. And against that threat the Chinese Christian Church is absolutely united with the whole of the Chinese people in resistance. As to the reality of germ warfare, there is no shadow of doubt in the mind of the Christian community; that was as evident in Canton as in Mukden itself.

The formal documents presented to me are three:

A Peace Call from the Hangchow Christian leaders dated June 13, 1952, and signed by eighteen distinguished Church leaders of various Christian communions, including Kimber S. K. Deng, Bishop of Chekiang Diocese.

A manifesto from 410 pastors and lay leaders of Protestant churches and organizations from Peking, Shanghai, and Tientsin, including four bishops of the Anglican Church and two bishops of the (American) Methodist Church.

A manifesto of the Roman Catholic Church in Peking, signed jointly by Chia Chen-ming, Chairman of the Chinese Catholic Church Reform Committee of Peking, and Li Chun-wu, Assistant Bishop of Peking Diocese, of the Chinese Roman Catholic Church. The signatories to this latter manifesto have amounted in a brief space of time to 13,755, including two bishops, two coadjutor bishops, 141 fathers and 130 priests, and 110 nuns.

A fourth document of a like nature has since come from Hankow.

The first two documents are beautifully written on parchment and bear the personal seal of each signatory.

In addition to these documents I will quote from the personal letter of Bishop T. Lindel Tsen, the doyen bishop of the Anglican Communion (now the Holy Catholic Church) of Shanghai:

"As to the fact of germ warfare. I have not been to Korea myself, but I have many personal friends and acquaintances who have been to Korea and northeast China for the purpose of investigating this most inhuman and un-Christian crime of the U.S. forces. Some of these investigators saw the germ-carriers, such as flies, mosquitoes, spiders, rats, and insects in patches moving on the glittering snow-covered ground at a season when usually such insects could not have existed. Moreover, some kinds of insects dropped down were foreign to that part of Korea. During their investigations some of them saw the actual dropping of such insects by the U.S. planes. Among the investigators I knew a pastor, Rev. T. C. Wong of the Congregational Church, Peking, Madame Si Teh-chuen, the widow of the late Christian General Feng, and Dr. C. C. Sin of the Seventh Day Adventists' Hospital. The integrity and character of these people has not been questioned, so their report has been accepted by the public as trustworthy and genuine.

"I have a son teaching physics in the College of Technology in northeast China. His wife wrote us twice that the people in her city were busy catching insects dropped by U.S. planes."

I might add that Dr. T. C. Wong, now Secretary of the Chinese Christian Reform Movement, had told me himself how, as he was investigating, a feather had alighted on his own arm. Carefully removed, it was at once taken to a laboratory and found to be germ-bearing.

I laid these documents before the leaders of the Christian churches in Great Britain.

6 Germ War and Genocide

WHY is germ warfare universally abhorred by the civilized world? Surely because of its genocidal aims, its intention to wipe out whole populations by disease. Such intention makes its use in China more understandable, though none the less inexcusable, in the hands of those who regard this quarter of the human race as so negligent of health and ignorant of the elements of cleanliness and sanitation that they would fall ready victims to the ravages of disease. If that is the intention, and if those are the credited Chinese characteristics, then China is an excellent target for the pseudo-science which thinks that world population is menacingly great and should be drastically reduced by any or every means.

The prime question for us, however, at the moment is: has germ warfare begun? That question can receive only one answer from any who have examined the evidence on the spot. I personally was convinced of the fact beyond any doubt, though I was careful, on my return, to lay little stress on my own conviction. I had gone to China to compare the old with the new. But while there I had been entrusted with a message from the whole Church of China, which was unanimous in its conviction and condemnation of U.S. germ warfare. It was that overwhelming evidence which broke through the silence at home and called forth bitter anger and ridicule. That evidence still stands and is unanswered. But I, as I said, was convinced personally, and the build-up of my positive conviction was as follows:

1. The weight of evidence of the Commission of International Lawyers, entrusted with the task of investigation by the International Association of Democratic Lawyers and led by Dr. Brandweiner, Roman Catholic Professor of International Law and Canon Law in Austria, whom I met in Czechoslovakia on his return from China. Their evidence of examination and cross-examination is published in full and also in summarized form in a monograph of 5,000 words.

This commission of eight eminent lawyers from Austria, Italy, France, Belgium, Brazil, and Poland, with Mr. Jack Gaster from Great Britain, having examined a large number of witnesses in a variety of places and heard and weighed the testimony of many bacteriological and other scientific experts, has published its imposing report. Summarizing their conclusions and noting the unusual presence of insects of unusual kinds, in unusual temperatures, carrying disease-producing microorganisms, and, in the nine cases examined, establishing the fact that American aircraft had flown over on the very same day, or a few days before, witnesses also having seen objects dropping from the planes, the members of commission unanimously agreed that the infected insects could only have been transported to these areas by American aircraft which had no right or reason to fly over northeastern Chinese territory at all. They considered that the acts reported constituted an aggression committed by the U.S.A., an act of genocide, a particularly odious crime against humanity, which presents to the world an exceedingly grave menace.

2. The Scientific Exhibitions at Peking and Mukden of everything relating to the evidence—places attacked, nature of attack, implements employed and found, insects, etc., dropped, with photographs of eyewitnesses and localities attacked and the methods of protection.

3. Conversations with leading bacteriologists, scientists, and physicians of the Eastern world, many of them Western-trained and of worldwide reputation, as, for example, Professor S. H. Chen, Doctor of Paris University, Chu Chi-ming, Doctor of Philosophy of Cambridge University,

At a small cottage in the lonely countryside we heard the simple stories, plain and clear, of the peasant farmer and his neighbours.

Wu Chi-chung, Fellow of the Royal Faculty of Physicians and Surgeons of Glasgow, etc.

4. My own investigations in three localities in northeast China.

On the spot, at the ruined concrete grandstand at the Fushan racecourse and at a small cottage in the lonely countryside (between Fushan and Mukden), we heard the simple stories, direct, plain, and clear, of the peasant farmer and his neighbors who had found scattered groups of strange insects on the snow on a cold March day. Most impressive, perhaps of all, to me, was the tale of Yang Hao-lung, a young Christian woman of the Irish Presbyterian Mission in Shanghai, who is now living in Mukden and was summoned to the spot—an ice-covered tennis court in a residential area of Mukden—when the sirens told of the low passage of a plane and summoned health workers to their posts. She had helped to collect the strange insects of unusual and unknown character, arriving in circumstances which could not be natural, and which caused at that time two cases of encephalitis (unknown there before) and convulsive death to two young children whose infected brains are carefully preserved in the nearby hospital laboratory.

The whole story of these attacks, of which this is but an incident, was vouched for and corroborated by the religious leaders in Mukden, with whom we held a long session.

The Reverend Sun Peng-hsi, General Secretary of the Northeast Synod of the Church of Christ in China, said in particular that he had found in his own yard flies unknown in this part of the country and in a temperature so cold that flies would not normally appear at all. The students and teachers at a nearby school were organized to round up these strange insects at this unwonted period.

The Reverend Wong Chen of the Church of Christ in China, the Reverend Kou Ching-kwang, also of the Church of Christ in China, Mr. Han Shih-chi, Chairman of the local Roman Catholic Church Reform Movement in China, and Miss Chow Peng-yien, Vice-Chairman of the local Roman Catholic Reform Movement Committee of Shenyang, also bore united and unanimous witness to the terrible reality and brutal nature of germ warfare in Mukden and northern China.

5. The evidence, to my mind impressive and conclusive, of two shot-down American airmen—Quinn and Enoch—given verbally and also recorded in their own handwriting in lengthy documents, which I saw, and, on gramophone records, which I heard.

6. The evidence of Mr. Wilfred Burchett, sometime correspondent in Central Europe for the *Daily Express,* who not only spoke at length with the two captured airmen, but was himself able to describe an air attack in June, the effects of which he himself had experienced, while he was visiting the U.S.A. Prisoner of War Camp on the Yalu River. Dropped in spherical receptacles which dissolved as they fell, the beehive-shaped mass of insects swarmed through the planks of Mr. Burchett's craft and up the banks of the river, where the Chinese guard buried them

in trenches with the help of American prisoners. One of these latter, skeptical of the germ theory, bit the head off an insect and swallowed it. Within twenty-four hours his temperature rose to 104 degrees, and he would have died but for the protection of inoculations previously administered to the U.S. forces.

7. The Report on Bacteriological Warfare presented by M. Yves Farge, President of the French Peace Movement, who went with the writer, Claude Roy, as delegate to Peking and stayed from April 28 to June 16, 1952, examining, with the aid of Professor Chen Wen-kwsi, one of the foremost Asian authorities on plague and former representative appointed by the League of Nations for the study of plague in India, and upward of fifty other scientific specialists and colleagues, the comprehensive facts, documents, and statements in connection with the raids in China and Korea.

M. Farge begins with the important and regulating principle that nothing should be described, calculated to aid the American General Staff responsible for the attacks. Two captured parachutists, Wang Ki and Ok Byong Fuk, had been given instructions to report the extent of the epidemics; to estimate the number of deaths; and to collect information on Chinese and Korean anti-epidemic measures. In view of this, Chinese and Korean military authorities would naturally wish to clamp down on all information; instead, they generally allowed the collection of sufficient information for scientific proof.

What impressed M. Farge at once was the massive apparatus of material for the defense of the population against the bacteriological offensive, contained in files into which every professor, doctor and research worker had put his best to arrive at rules and means of defense most adequate to frustrate attack.

M. Farge brought with him the following declaration signed by fifty-two Chinese scientists: "We have accumulated enough scientific proof to establish that the American forces have in fact employed bacteriological warfare in Korea and in our country."

M. Farge was convinced of the truth of this declaration and justified his positive attitude by showing at length the data leading to the following conclusions:

"There is in existence a concerted and studied plan controlling the development of the bacterial war, and this plan has become apparent during its course.

"The essential aspects of the unfolding of the attack coincide with the military and scientific data published in the United States, in books, periodicals, newspapers, and reports.

"The laboratory findings in Korea and China corroborate the admissions of prisoners, even though these admissions contain scientific heresies.

"Biological warfare as now being waged must be looked on as a stage in a sequence of atrocities, a stage which may lead to the use of atomic devices whose presence near the theater of operations is known."

The documents, the witnesses, the regions examined, together with the presence of the four laboratories fully equipped with the best German, Japanese, and U.S. apparatus, present an imposing array of evidence.

The U.S. attack had demonstrably been prolonged, scientific, and thorough, a complete "try-out," to solve the problems of the widest possible artificial dispersal of pathogenic agents by wind, leaves, feathers, paper, or insignificant objects a passerby might put in his pocket. Questions had arisen: *e.g.* the significance of the meat or dead animals dropped. The cases carefully examined and collected showed that these had been scattered to provide a suitable breeding ground for the attendant flies, bearing intestinal infections. Similarly, leaves were observed to be scattered in areas where silkworms are reared or cotton grown, to destroy crops with pathogenic fungus, to kill them in order to starve or to disrupt man's industry. Efforts had been made to poison sea-water and fresh-water reservoirs: the first act of health squads had been, in consequence, to empty reservoirs, condemn them, and then mobilize the entire population involved to put chloramine in all drinking water.

Massive data collected show that the bacteriological tactics are mainly directed against roads, inhabited areas, and lines of communication. Air operations against springs and streams of water in northeast China had little effect, because to eliminate the least chance of the plague reappearing in Manchuria the population had already been trained to drink no water not previously boiled or otherwise disinfected.

The picture grows clearer with the data collected. For example, the scattering of flies and fleas on ruins in Korea and China in wintertime is based on the fact that these insects creep into dark holes and crannies, to emerge among the population later.

Some hundreds of plague-infected voles had been found in Manchuria after U.S. planes had flown over, in regions which had never yet known plague, either among men or animals.

Against those who suggest that diseases unknown in the north were imported by south Chinese is the fact that simultaneously, and in many places, the same type of infected objects, black spring-tail, big housefly, spiders carrying typhoid bacillus, etc., appeared in Korea and north China.

M. Farge naturally finds the evidence of the two captured airmen, U.S. First Lieutenant John Quinn and First Lieutenant Kenneth Enoch, of great importance, together with that of another, Marvin L. Brown.

The statements of these men were full and detailed, giving data which could easily be refuted or contradicted and could be known only to the inner circle of the U.S. Air force. They were given freely and confirmed in private conversation.

Since M. Farge's visit, further valuable evidence has been obtained from Second Lieutenant Floyd B. O'Neal, First Lieutenant C. O. Armstrong, and First Lieutenant Paul R. Kniss, captured U.S. airmen. Their statements are highly detailed, describing training and instructions.

Lieutenant O'Neal states that in his opinion it was apparent that the American forces had chosen wintertime to start using bacteriological weapons for the purpose of using Korea as a try-out ground to test the cold-withstanding bacteriological weapons developed in special laboratories. The final purpose was to use them in bacteriological warfare against countries with cold climates, such as the Soviet Union and the People's Democracies.

O'Neal testified that the American forces had urged germ warfare for over a year, even while peace talks were in progress.

It is, added O'Neal, a hard thing for a pilot to do, dropping these germs on innocent citizens . . . but he has no choice. . . . The use of germ warfare is against all humanitarian principles. . . Americans should speak out and condemn those who made the decision to use this weapon.

There appeared to the certain contradictions between the evidence of Kniss and O'Neal, both of the 18th Fighter Bomber group, both flying F51's and both briefed by Captain McLaughlin.

Both agree that:

1. They were briefed by McLaughlin.
2. The methods to be used were V.T. bombs for germs, etc.
3. There was need for secrecy, etc.

Points of disagreement are:

1. O'Neal was told it would not matter much whether the V.T. bombs exploded in the air or on the ground, that the bacteria would survive in

any case, whereas Kniss was told that the explosion would kill the bacteria if the bomb hit the ground. . . .

2. Kniss was warned not to fly at over 12,000 feet in case the germs were killed through lack of oxygen. O'Neal was not given this warning.

3. O'Neal was told to drop bombs over towns or areas with large troop concentrations, Kniss to drop them 5 to 10 kilometers outside towns. Why this discrepancy? Kniss was briefed two months after O'Neal. The Americans must have realized that germ warfare was not providing the results expected. The Americans had learned by three months' experience that germ warfare was not so simple as they thought. Decontamination measures taken had made it useless to drop germs on towns.

4. O'Neal was told to drop bombs in some uninhabited spot in South Korea if prevented from dropping them in North Korea. Kniss was told to keep them aboard and return to base, possibly because of a "mysterious" outbreak of typhus in a remote South Korean mountain village.

5. O'Neal describes spraying missions in February; Kniss was told they would not take place before June.

6. Kniss was forced to sign a secrecy statement not required by O'Neal. The publicity concerning germ warfare received by March 21, was being discussed at the air bases. The necessity to stop discussion was more urgent on March 21 than on January 22, when O'Neal was briefed.

We cannot but conclude that the discrepancies merely reflect the modification of methods introduced by the Americans as they developed their germ war plans.

Since then has come the Report of the International Scientific Commission, composed of distinguished European, South American, and Indian scientists, assembled by invitation and reaching China in mid-June, 1952.

China and Korea had refused to accept investigations by the World Health Organization, since this was a specialized agency of the United Nations, whose flag was being used by the American forces charged with the crime.

They had likewise refused to accept investigations by the so-called International Red Cross. As regards this body, it was pointed out that there exists in reality no "International Red Cross." The "International Committee of the Red Cross," which it was proposed should make investigations, is in fact a committee of the Swiss Red Cross and the word "international" refers only to its activities and not to its composition.

Moreover, this was the body which "investigated" Auschwitz during the Second World War, and never exposed or challenged the atrocities which are known to have been perpetrated there; and recently it also "investigated" the Koje Prisoner of War Camp at the time of the illegal screening of prisoners there, and again raised no adequate protest. It could not, therefore, inspire the least confidence as an investigating agency.

The International Scientific Commission was composed of eminent scientists from Sweden, France, Italy, Brazil, the U.S.S.R., with, as its British representatives, Dr. Joseph Needham, F.R.S., and Sir William Dunn, Reader in Bio-chemistry of Cambridge University and formerly scientific Counselor of H. B. M. Embassy, Chungking, and later Director of the Department of Natural Sciences, U.N.E.S.C.O.

The recently published sixty-one-page monograph, together with a list of forty-six appendices, is the precursor of the immense 300,000-word document containing the fully detailed evidence. Both documents now lie before me.

The careful labor of the Commission is what one would expect of scientists of worldwide repute. I met Dr. Needham in Peking before he joined the investigating party. He was singularly critical and outlined what he would demand as evidence. The findings of the Commission that "the people of Korea and China have indeed been the objective of bacteriological weapons" and that "these have been employed by units of the U.S. armed forces, using a great variety of different methods for the purpose, some of which seem to be developments of those applied by the Japanese Army during the Second World War," are conclusive for serious-minded students. The more so as these conclusions, "reached by passing from one logical step to another," were reached with reluctance, "the Commission members being indisposed to believe that such inhuman technique could have been put into execution in face of its universal condemnation by the peoples of the nations."

This weighty evidence, packed into sixty pages, is most impressive. It records travels far and wide through North Korea and northeast China. It contains a careful comparison with the relevant data concerning Japanese use of germ warfare in World War II, together with detailed medical notes on the insects disseminated, and on plant-destroying organisms. It examines very closely the outbreak of plague in Korea, where there had been no plague for five centuries, and in the month of February, three months too early for its normal appearance in any such climate. It examines cases of anthrax, etc., and explains in detail the large variety of germ-containers used and the many methods of their dissemination.

More important than all these factors of evidence, however, it interviewed at length one of the captured intelligence agents, and most important of all, it interviewed, as Farge had done, and at still greater length, the captured airmen, Quinn, Enoch, Brown, and, in addition, Armstrong. These officers had attended secret lectures on methods of bacteriological warfare. They had received orders to carry out bacteriological warfare. They had done so with the greatest inner reluctance.

"With these four American airmen, two more, Lieutenant F. B. O'Neal and Lieutenant Paul Kniss, whose accounts were even more lengthy and detailed, had subsequently been captured, the Commission found itself in a good cross-section of American life—a cool-headed electrical engineer, a middle class businessman, a young research chemist, and a solid steel-mill worker of agricultural origin." It had opportunities for long conversations. It was unanimously of the opinion that no pressure, physical or mental, had been brought to bear on these prisoners of war in order to induce them to make the declarations which were made.

"This confidence in the physical and mental stability of the airmen makes the more significant their frank words of regret for their part in germ warfare.

"These declarations were made of their own free will, after long experience of the friendliness and kindness of their Chinese and Korean captors had brought to them the realization that their duty to all races and people must outweigh their natural scruples at revealing what might be considered the military secrets of their own Government."

The substance of the interviews is reproduced as an appendix. "From their written statements and answers to questions it seems already possible to reconstruct what was going on in the American Air Force during the last months of 1951 and the early months of 1952."

It is noted that these airmen did not remember ever having received any instructions on the recognized customs and usages of war, such as the prohibition of the shooting of prisoners, nor of having seen the regulations relating thereto in American Manuals of Procedure; still less had they heard of the outlawing of certain forms of war, at least by certain nations. All were unanimous on the disastrous effects on the morale of men ordered to conduct germ warfare. "It was the last straw for many of them, already disgusted by the ferocity with which they were being hounded on to slaughter the civilian population of North Korea."

The Commission concludes that "they have every reason to accept the veracity and to uphold the integrity of the officers who gave evidence before it. They appeared to be fully normal and in perfect health, they spoke in a natural way and seemed fully at their ease. . . . The Commission therefore accepts as true and faithful the evidence of the airmen, which complemented indeed in many ways the strictly scientific observational evidence already accumulated."

To all this massive evidence the voice of the united Christian Churches of China, as set forth in the previous chapter, is a clinching voice.

7 National and Small-Scale Capitalism

CHINA is semi-socialist and, for a simple reason, likely to remain so for a considerable time. China lacks large-scale industry, but needs the products of industry and needs them in rapidly increasing quantities. It would be wholly impracticable therefore to socialize every small-scale industry and handicraft industry at once. Impracticable even to socialize all of the large-scale capitalist industry. All that is possible and necessary at the present time is to control capitalist industry, to see that it acts in accordance with the new demands for workers' safety, standards of life, and security in case of sickness, ill-health, and old age.

This is already assured. And there is a further guarantee against danger from such capitalism as remains. The Chinese People's Republic had, as soon as the Japanese and Kuomintang had departed, taken over large numbers of industrial units which had been in their hands. To digest and organize all these is sufficient task for the present. Shortage of skilled technicians to administer them supplies a check. Non-socialist technicians were perforce employed, with results not always or wholly satisfactory. That difficulty, however, is met. Free university courses are now provided to supply a large and regular flow of technicians to industry, as well as of doctors and teachers to the professions. But the process takes time.

In the meantime, the present large-scale socialist industry, running side by side with large-scale and small-scale capitalist industry, acts as check and counter-check. In precisely the same way the large-scale socialist stores and shops act as a check upon capitalist and individualist stores and shops. When prices drop in one, prices perforce must drop in the others; when conditions are good in the one, they must be good in the others; or competition will drive them out of business.

Hence these two forms of industrial life run at present side by side. And the national capitalist industrialists and the small-scale industrialists have nothing to complain of in the new set-up. They are supplied with unlimited markets. The new spending power of the peasants creates an immense demand for goods, more at times than the factories can cope with, especially considering the effects of the blockade. Hence industrial units, both socialist and capitalist, expand to meet the new demands, every care being taken to prevent the capitalist section of the industrial world from running away and getting out of public control. Control is kept complete.

What the future of China's petty handicraft will be is not easy to forecast. Its present scale is enormous. Much of it is beautiful. Much of it is efficient.

Doubtless much will be taken over, as in the capitalist world, by large-scale units and turned over to mass production, with its benefits of cheapness, but with its danger from the artistic point of view.

And there will always be the check provided by the growing socialist and collective habits of mind, to correct tendencies to individualism in production and to effect the transition from capitalism to socialism wherever and whenever possible. The enormous benefits of collective work on the big scale in the water conservation schemes, or in teamwork on farms, is creating in China, as it has already more thoroughly created in Russia by the astounding success of her recent gigantic schemes, an interest in, and a leaning towards, large-scale collective industry. There is, in short, no fear in which direction China will move in respect to any of her branches of industrial activity, large or small. The trend will be nearer and nearer to socialism and, that achieved, to communism.

8 Transport Carries Prosperity

WE had bananas in Peking in June, 1952, and missed them in Canton, where they grow. "Why?" I asked. "Bananas are common food, not fitting for guests," was the reply. We ate bananas again in Mukden. Nothing very extraordinary in that, you say. Perhaps not, but very revealing to anyone who knew the wreckage of China's railways in 1949.

For the first time, indeed, in thirteen years China's major trunk lines were working on January 1, 1950. The task of restoration has been colossal. It is now complete. Many lines had ceased operation since the Japanese occupation; rails carted away, ties used as firewood, roadbeds leveled and planted with crops. Lines everywhere had deteriorated through the Kuomintang's negligence: bridges and tunnels were blown sky high as the Kuomintang retreated. Forty percent of sleepers needed replacement, 80 percent of locomotives, 40 percent of passenger carriages, and 25 percent of freight cars were short in the northeast. Worse still was the destruction in south China. Every large bridge along the Canton-Hankow Railway had been blown up.

"Where the People's Army goes, the trains must go," said Mao Tse-tung. Repair of rail communications was, therefore, given high priority in 1948. From January 15 to March 3, 1949, 1,080 kilometers of rail line were repaired; north China was linked with northeast China; 4,475 kilometers more repaired between April and October, 1949; by the end of 1949 another 2,655. By January 1, 1950, 21,046 kilometers of China's total network of 29,922 kilometers were in regular use.

Prodigious feats of engineering were performed. As we sailed on the Huai River in June, 1952, I looked up at the great bridge of the Tientsin-Pukow Railway. I had seen post-war photographs of the bridge, every span sent crashing to the river bed. It had been completely rebuilt in two months. It took thirty days only to rebuild the Hsian River Bridge along the Hunan-Kwangsi-Kweichon line: the Kuomintang had tried in vain to rebuild it in four years. Again, why? The whole people were behind the rebuilding of a bridge they now owned. Every engineering workshop in the land had vied to provide material to reconstruct China's vital transport lines. Peasants hauled sleepers and rails from caves and jungles where they had hidden them. Workers had surpassed themselves for speed when they relaid 12 kilometers of track in one day and repaired 45 metres of bridge on another.

All this means much to me, or to anyone else who has studied the food situation in China at times of famine.

In 1932 I stood beside a missionary friend and saw the famished refugees. The same friend told me how in the previous year he had faced a crowd of starving peasants immediately after the great flood and famine of 1931. He had received from the International Famine Relief Fund supplies of grain, but only enough to feed half the multitude. He faced the agonizing choice: Which half?

"Not," he said, "that there was no grain in China." There was sufficient with the supplies that were pouring in. What was lacking was transport for the grain. Roads and railways were a prime essential in times of famine, and China lacked both.

It was that situation which had prompted the Famine Relief Fund to build a highway through Kansu, a task entrusted to Major Todd. When I left him, his handsome graded road was partially finished, even to surmounting the high Lupin San range in graceful easy gradients. That road now forms part of the great highway which runs through Sinkiang to Russia.

Transport had always been a primary need of China, hence my enthusiasm at the rapid reconstruction of China's railroads, an enthusiasm still further stimulated by the efficiency of the day-to-day working of Chinese railways and by the mighty new rail constructions. In some 6,000 or 7,000 miles' rail travel in 1952 I never knew a Chinese train to be late and never saw a dirty carriage or a dirty station.

The cleanliness needs to be seen to be believed. Carriages are perpetually dusted and corridors perpetually swabbed. Flies, if they appear at all, are swatted at once.

Women have speedily taken their place in the railway services. A standard has been set by the "Women's Special" which runs between Peking and Tientsin. Drivers, stokers, guards, are all women. The locomotive is called "International Women's Day." The woman guards help the children and the aged, pack luggage on the racks, swab the corridors directly the train leaves the station.

China's transport facilities, shipping, highways, and railways, as a whole, form a fascinating and illuminating theme of study.

Shipping had been developed by foreign powers and had remained under foreign control for a hundred years. There is truth in the charge that it carried little to China except cheap surplus goods—which impoverished China's farmers by displacing their wives' handicraft work, an indispensable addition to the farmers' own beggarly earnings—and sidetracked China's own industrial development.

The returning ships carried off to the Western world much of China's raw material wealth, and the many fruits of her cheap labor.

Such inland highways as China possessed were built largely for military purposes, and useful mainly for foreign penetration, with small regard for the needs of China's millions. China's railways were few and utterly insufficient for China's needs, with freight rates both anti-social and full of ridiculous anomalies.

The Liberation Government brought speedy change. Shipping passed into Chinese hands, with recovery of all navigation rights, and abolition of the one-sided arrangements enabling foreign vessels to dominate coastwise and river trade. The Liberation Government took over wharves and storehouses, bringing all establishments and administrations under the people's control. Coastwise routes were reopened. Inland water routes were improved and extended to a length of 35,340 miles. Besides the rehabilitation of twenty good harbors, a new and vast harbor is under construction at Tientsin to bring ocean-going ships alongside the wharf at Tangku, the seaport of Tientsin. On the Yangtze River the great wharf at Pukow, which was in peril of collapse, has been made secure by dredging operations which have divided the river into two main channels. Sunk or damaged ships have been salvaged. Shipping in 1951 was 139 percent greater than at the time of the Liberation.

Inland waterways, so important for transport in China, have been lengthened and deepened as, for example, on the Huai River, and pressed into strenuous service to supply the need of expanding industry, expanding agriculture, and vast construction tasks. Millions were fed at the Huai River Project and on the Yellow River by rice shipped down the Yangtze and up the Huai River itself. And it was Chinese ships that took grain to India in 1951.

Chinese inland shipping, which has now a continuous task in promoting trade between town and countryside, works according to a plan, which makes it possible to gauge progress or the reverse. In 1950 it achieved 104 percent of its set target for that year, in 1951 maritime transport fulfilled 142 percent of its plan.

Freight charges are only 12 percent of former levels, harbor dues are reduced from 50 to 6. Water transport, inland and external, has been radically transformed.

Construction of new railroads, however, is the outstanding transport fact which grips the Chinese imagination, the new Szechuan railway being an outstanding illustration.

The railway from Chungking, the capital, to Chengfu, the leading agricultural town of this rich and vast province, as large as Germany, existed on the drawing boards in Manchu days. Save for a few short strips of line here and there and a station or two never used, the Chungking railway remained a blueprint all through the Kuomintang days. It only emerged as a mighty reality under the People's Government.

The total distance from Chungking, Szechuan's commercial and industrial center, to Chengfu, its rich agricultural center, is 319 miles, longer than the distance from London to Carlisle. The whole line has been completed in record time and is now in operation.

Driving the first spike in June, 1950, a regular service was running to Yungchuan, 102 miles distant, by July, 1951, to Neiking, 175 miles distant, by December, 1951, and so on.

The terrain, traversing mountains and rivers, necessitating 40 tunnels and 970 bridges, was intensely daunting. One tunnel of 812 yards pierced solid rock. Graceful bridges and turns, built on a curve, span deep and difficult gorges.

Yet this line was built by the Chinese themselves, mainly by the Liberation Army, aided by 100,000 local workers under technical direction of a handful of Chinese engineers.

It was a devoted band with the whole country engineering on their behalf behind them and eagerly following every mile of advance. Material of every kind poured in from every corner of China's vast territory, the local people supplying local stone and timber.

The new railway brings prosperity to farm and factory, to sugar farms, tool shops, cement works, and brick fields over large areas of Szechuan, speeding the realization of its vast potential wealth.

This smoothest and best-built line in all China is in a very real sense the people's line. The whole nation is proud of it. It takes its rightful place beside the other outstanding achievements of the past three years of Liberation rule.

9 Agricultural Giant, Industrial Infant

THE Liberation found agricultural China a giant and industrial China a feeble infant. That was due to deliberate policy. As a result of imperialist domination of the country, modern industry was lamentably undeveloped. Even in 1937, on the eve of the war with Japan, the total number of working lathes in the whole country was only about 90,000. Ninety thousand for a population twice the size of Western Europe!

Iron and steel production, about 2,500,000 tons.

Electric power output, 2,000,000 kilowatts; Textile spindles, 5,000,000.

China was a nation of handicraft industry and gigantic agriculture. Such modern industry as existed was more or less dependent on foreign capital. China repeated the pattern of all semi-colonial economies.

A similar policy indeed molds the economies of the Middle East today. Dominated or influenced for many decades by imperialist powers and policies, Egypt, Turkey, Iraq and Iran have been subtly engineered, not only to be and remain agricultural, but to develop an agriculture most suited to the imperialist interests, suited to imperialist needs for raw materials and food requirements: Egypt a monocultural country, cotton practically her only crop; Turkey predominantly tobacco-producing; Iraq dates; Iran rice and cotton: no balance between agriculture and industry, not even agricultural balance with varied crops. Egypt's cotton areas were expanded by cutting down other crops, notably cereals, which she must now import, as does also Iran.

It is an economy highly dangerous to the countries involved. It is the inevitable cause of the notorious and deplorable low standard of living from which their peasantry suffer. So it was with China.

Take cotton. China can grow cotton; China can spin cotton; China can weave cotton. But the foreign hold on China's cotton was tight, tight too on China's textile industry. The infant cotton industry was hit by imperialism at birth and many subsequent times in the course of its development. Cotton, the raw material for the textile industry, grows, and grows well, in China, but it served foreign interests better to keep China to simpler cultures, food cultures, so much so that in recent decades raw cotton has been imported, culminating in Chiang Kai-shek's collaboration with American imperialism after V-J Day, whereby huge quantities of cotton every year have been imported. Cotton production in China declined, forced out by cheap, dumped foreign cotton, and the Chinese textile industry was forced in addition to rely on imperialist combines for its supply of raw materials.

Worse even than that, China, owing to the growing poverty of the peasantry became dependent upon foreign markets for the sale of its finished textile goods. After the Japanese War, 20 percent of China's finished goods was transported to colonial countries under imperialist control, to the detriment of the industry. Mill-owners likewise suffered through post-war inflation. They let management decline and took instead to speculation. The textile industry remained a dwarfed, semi-starved, infant industry, and agriculture an impoverished giant.

But the Liberation enriched the gaint and had a double effect on the textile industry. As agricultural China grew richer, more money accumulated in the pockets of millions of purchasers who needed new cotton clothes. Here was an immense market for the coarser linens, though perhaps with a diminution in demand for the finer luxury lines upon which the textile industry had hitherto been obliged to rely. In the shops at Shanghai in June, 1952, we saw range after range of these cheap, brightly colored prints: the little girls of China turn out gay to deck the streets and fields with color. Furthermore, the agriculturalist is provided with a stable and paying market for homegrown cotton.

The textile cotton industry then is transformed by these three factors:

1. China grows her own excellent cotton.
2. The purchasing power of 145 million households has risen and provides ample market for textile goods.
3. Mismanagement is eliminated both by example of State-owned factories and also by providing the private manufacturer with a stable price and a good market. No longer is he driven to speculation.

Hence production figures leap ahead. In 1950 the plan for cotton yarn was 21.12 percent overfulfilled. Cloth production also reached its peak. The boon is twofold. The industry flourishes and the masses can wear low-priced, durable, and attractive clothing. Thus encouraged, the plan for yarn and cloth in 1951 provided for an increase of 33 percent over 1950, or 28 percent above the highest level ever before reached in the Chinese textile industry. The cotton-growing area increased by 280 percent. Cotton-growing, though formerly presenting more difficulties than grain and more precarious, has become increasingly popular, because more profitable and aided by the Government, which has allotted a reasonable ratio between cotton prices and grain prices. Water conservation also has added many hundreds of thousands of irrigated acres to increase production both of cotton and of grain.

As with the textile industry, so with textile machinery. During the sixty years of China's textile industry, China's mills have been dependent upon foreign imports for all their textile machinery. The few textile machine plants that existed never made textile machines; they only assembled and repaired them.

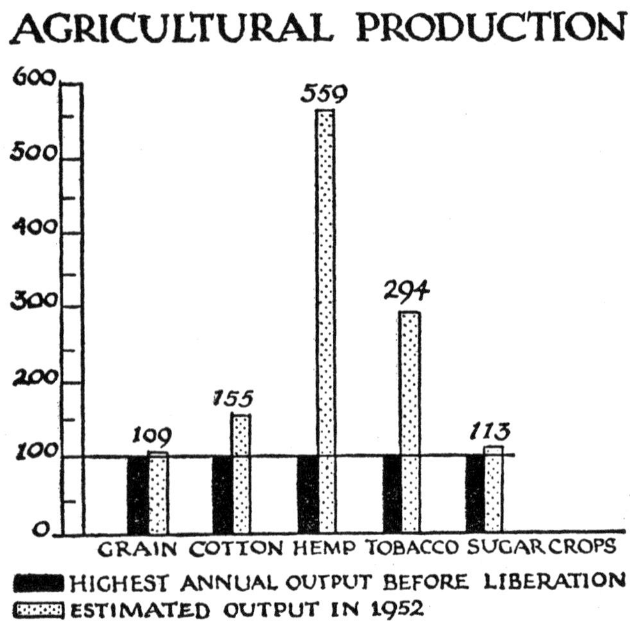

But by the spring of 1951 a plan for machine production, standardized as a step to mass production, was launched. Demands for supplies were urgent; by spring, 1952, the contemporary needs were met through a threefold increase in production of spindles and a twofold increase in loom production over 1951. Adequate steps are taken besides this for the demands which are bound to come as the textile industry expands.

Another important and illuminating development is seen in the jute mills of Hangchow. Sacks are made of jute. Jute came from India. The American blockade cut off China's jute supplies. But jute-made sacks are essential for grain carriage and storage in China.

The dilemma drove China to create and develop her own jute industry.

The Kuomintang had in 1938 ordered and received a unit of jute machinery from Messrs. Fairbairn, Lawson, Coombe and Barbour of Leeds and Belfast. The Kuomintang had left it to rust. It was unearthed in May, 1950, cleaned, some 2,000 damaged or missing parts replaced, and installed in a factory at Hangchow and was operating on August 1. A duplicate machine made in Chinese shops by Chinese engineers, and fitted with many improvements, chiefly in the spinning sheds, with lower machines, suited to the lower stature of Chinese girls, was running in June, 1952. We also saw an immense new factory shed for other Chinese-made jute machines, eight times the size of the original. This was in Hangchow alone. China now grows her own jute staple, longer and better than that from India. The American blockade has provided China with her own independently-made jute sacks, to the benefit of farmers and industrialists alike.

Incidentally, that jute factory is an embellishment to Hangchow—a city noted for its singular beauty—and a model for mill establishments. No factory smoke fouls the air. The building, excellently designed and constructed, stands amid gardens and flowerbeds with creches, lavatories, dining rooms and a library paved with an admirably fitted parquet floor. Amid beautiful surroundings are grouped the hostel houses, where young men and women can live, with lodging and board, for one third of their weekly wage.

Fertilizers, though something new in China's agriculture, are another growing industry. China's soil is twice the area of Europe's soil. The importance of fertilizers for its cultivation is obvious. Chinese farmers with their new purchasing power cán now buy them, and are eager to do so, especially fertilizers are essential to high-quality cotton production. The national larder and adequate supply of raw materials depend on fertilizers. Consequently, decisive steps are taken to develop this vital industry. It is a priority, and already by 1952, despite shocking neglect during the Kuomintang regime, the output exceeds the highest pre-Liberation period by 25 percent.

China's inherited roads demand Chinese-made jeeps. Her rough mud tracks, branching far and wide across farm lands, lack the smooth surface of English tar-macadamed country lanes. They demand jeeps. And at Tientsin in the great North China Exhibition in 1951 people crowded round to see China's first Chinese-made jeep. Tractors now produced by workers in Taiyuan, Shansi Province, were also shown at the Exhibition.

In that same Tientsin Exhibition were exhibits of over 100 machine items of major importance, including coal-cutting machinery for mines, automatic universal precision lathes, and a variety of other modern machine tools, together with 100-h.p. Diesel engines and electric trolley buses, which China was never able to make before. These trolley buses and jeeps were especially interesting because, again, it was due to American action, to American refusal to allow Japan to send to China the buses, or indeed any other articles, she had ordered for use in Tientsin. The reaction of the engineers of Shanghai was: "We can make them." And make them they did with the same skill that they produced the trolley buses in Tientsin and Mukden.

A peasant lingering around a mechanical oil-press at the Exhibition remarked: "It does the work of the four mules that we use for the job in our village and it costs a lot less." And he might have added it sets free for other crops the land providing mule fodder. Here again is another intriguing peasant remark after viewing the Exhibition and, for the first time, seeing some of Tientsin's great factories: "We peasants thought we could make everything we were likely to need, except salt. We grew our own food, spun and wove our own cotton, produced our own vegetable oil for cooking and lamps. But now we see a much better future ahead of us, and we can't get there behind a wooden plow and an ox. However hard we try, we can't grow telephones and electric light."

The old days of Chinese agriculture are going fast, the days that were epitomized in the saying: "You don't need skill in farming. All you need is sweat." It is science, not sweat, which grows enormous melons and cabbages and the large-grained wheat.

The old Chinese saying that "Three shoe-makers make a sage," had a new application in the making of China's first jeep. When the Tientsin Automobile Assembly Plant began the process of making a jeep instead of the mere assemblage of parts, it found that much was lacking. Tools were lacking, parts were lacking, skill was lacking. But the will to make and the ingenuity of the workers were present in abundance, and they won their way through to success.

I had always held, twenty years ago, that Chinese workers were second to none in craft skill and that, given a chance with modern machines, they would soon learn the technique and be able before long to lead and not to follow. I had watched craftsmen of all sorts working in village

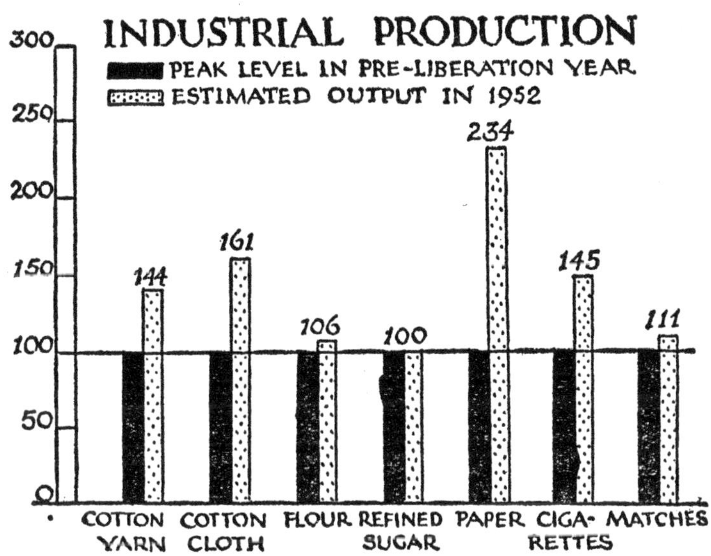

shops. I had examined tools and processes. I saw, for instance, a carpenter sawing through a narrow lath on a narrow trestle for bench and without a suspicion of splitting or chatter. I asked if I might examine his saw, which looked like a hatchet with a long, narrow blade. It was a very narrow blade, thin as cardboard, and so wide that it needed no heavy rib, like our tenon saws, to strengthen it. But the teeth! Never had I seen such teeth. Retrenchant teeth. Teeth like fish-hooks each turning back and curling over to a point like a curling-wave. Sharp as a razor. And the cut is a draw-cut, not a push-cut. Yet there was no chatter and the cut line was as straight as a die and the speed of the cutting astonishing.

I saw this same skill everywhere. Hence I marveled not at the improved jute machine or the thousand and one new invented devices springing up in Chinese industry. The workers of China, no longer bound by craft secrecy, pool their experiences. The assembly workers at Tientsin preparing to make the new jeeps and automobiles produced no less than 8,455 suggestions in the first seven months.

The price of essential machinery to the peasant drops owing to a new price relationship, which, doing no ill-service to the producer, gives big price reductions to the peasant purchaser.

Indeed, price drops take place all along the line.

"I worked in this shop for over twenty years before Liberation, but I never saw prices drop before. Each time I used to mark up the prices in the window, I worried as to how I could feed and clothe my own family," said Hsiang Chien-hua, a Shanghai shop clerk as he marked down item after item by an average of 11 percent. He added, "I never thought I would see this day."

A "golden dragon" fountain pen, for example, which previously cost $3.25, was marked down to $2.25. A pair of cotton stockings went down from 70 to 35 cents.

Industrial and consumer goods production show ever-advancing figures, and the advance is bound to increase as China with her vast potentialities gets under way. Let these graphs on pages 131 and 133 illustrate the constant upward trend of production.

10 Industry Booms in Manchuria, the Ruhr of Asia

CHINA'S major industrial deficiency is in the field of heavy industry, iron, coal and steel. There, then, is one of China's major problems, for coal and iron, and steel form the absolutely essential basis for industrializing any country. It need, however, have been no problem at all, for nothing, except foreign imperialist control and the greed of China's ruling classes, prevented China from becoming a leader in the industrial world.

For China is lavishly endowed by nature with raw materials of every kind. Indeed, if there is one place above all others where natural material riches appear in concentrated form, it is in the great northeast, in Manchuria and beyond.

Manchuria is singularly ill-known in the West, although germ warfare, the bombing of the great hydroelectric power station on the Yalu River, and the U.S.A.'s eagerness to advance beyond the 38th Parallel have at last focused the eyes of the world on her vast spaces. As big as Germany,

Italy, and Japan combined, Manchuria has all the potentialities of becoming one of the major industrial centers of the world. Already, and despite all hindrances and obstructions, coal production in Manchuria, according to statistics compiled in 1943, constituted 40 percent of the nation's output, pig iron 87 percent, finished steel products 93 percent, and electric power 78 percent. Railroad mileages account for 42 percent of the nation's total mileage.

No wonder covetous imperialist eyes fastened on Manchuria. No wonder they still fasten on Manchuria. No less wonder, also, that even before the American-backed Kuomintang Army had been driven from the area, Chairman Mao and the Central Committee of the Communist Party had determined to develop Manchurian industry in the interests of the Chinese people.

For lying hidden beneath the ground of Manchuria are an estimated 20 billion tons of coal. Seams and ore of coal and gold are apparent everywhere in Manchuria. Her iron deposits can yield 500 million tons of pig iron. Southwest Manchuria possesses what are reckoned to be the largest magnesite deposits in the world. Lead, zinc, copper, tin, aluminum, platinum, nickel, chrome, manganese, tungsten, molybdenum, phosphorus, and many other minerals have been discovered in workable quantities, together with shale oil and petroleum. Nothing is lacking of the material bases of industry.

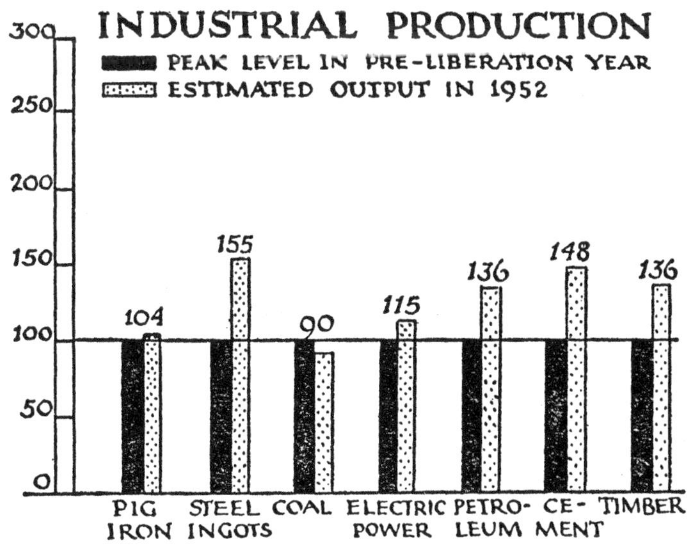

It is natural, then, that northern industry, with its heavy iron and steel production, rivals the light textile industry and jute industries of the center in vigor of development and speed of growth. Production in the whole of northeast China booms. Targets are high, but targets are reached. China knows, every individual in China knows, the Chinese Government knows, the paramount need for development of heavy industry: coal, iron, and steel. All know that Manchuria must be made the base for industrializing the whole of China.

But this, though known, is no easy task to achieve. The Liberation Government had inherited a wrecked and ruined industrial machine. Japan was not interested in long-term investments and took good care to crush any industrial development which might prove dangerously competitive to her own industry. The Kuomintang, when it succeeded Japan, had left matters worse than when they had found them, only intent on making hay while the sun shone.

Thus when the Liberation Government took over it found "an unevenly developed colonial type of industrial structure that had been slashed and gutted by the Kuomintang." Industrial production had fallen to less than half the 1949 level, the year previous to the Japanese departure.

That was the inheritance. But the potentialities were all there, the material deposits, an industrial framework, and, best of all, an eager, enthusiastic, hard-working, forward-looking people—workers who had fought in the last days of Japan and the Kuomintang against sabotage, who had hidden away vital elements of machines and, when hand tools were short, had contributed their own, and who worked with muscle and brain to build up China's great industrial base and reform China's whole economy.

The Liberation Government had other assets. Since the Kuomintang Government had kept most of the confiscated industry in its own hands, while ruining the remaining private industry with corrupt practices, the Liberation Government was able to control directly six-sevenths of the whole area's productive capacity and could therefore guide Manchuria's industrial development along lines most beneficial to the mass of the people.

Recovery, therefore, thanks to all these factors, was extremely rapid. By 1948 prices were becoming stabilized, communities were restored, trade, rural and national, re-established, spending money ampler among farmers and industrialists owing to land reform, wage control, and tax revision. Northeast China balanced her budget and wiped out her deficit.

We visited the engineering workshops in Mukden and the coal mines of Fushan, descending the 1,200-foot shaft at the chief pit. We studied the data of production and heard the story of the rescue of the pit from sabotage and of the defeat of the Kuomintang. As to the efficiency of the pit, I give the estimate of an expert British miner, a delegate at China's May Day festivities, whom we met in Peking. The conditions at Fushan were superior, he said, to any he had known at home: no dust, no silicosis; the workers descended to the coal face by a lift like that in our hotel, separate from the shaft where the coal was raised.

The pit itself is worked by machinery of the most modern type. Pit electric trains hold 3 tons apiece and the winding gear raises 12 tons at a time. The "bore hole and the blow" was the method worked in this pit on account of the slope. The seam itself was "terrific," 120 feet thick.

Pit rivals pit and coal field coal field in the effort to increase production. The methods of the winners are widely published and eagerly adopted; they lead to higher wages and a rising standard of living for all. For example, by means of new methods of tunneling at the State-owned Tatung Colliery in Charhan Province, ten miners created a new national tunneling record of 479 meters in thirty days. Using pneumatic drills and led by Ma Lu-hai, a national labor hero, they invented a method by which time lost in dynamiting was eliminated. It was the result of much pooled experience and several weeks of experiments, and it is now publicized among miners in all parts of the country and is bound to yield results in increased production.

Despite the destruction by the Kuomintang, and operating with 50 percent less equipment than in 1944, coal production had by 1949 reached 87 percent of the 1944 peak, when 25,300,000 tons were extracted, illustrating the change from driven-worker status to owner-worker status.

The average daily coal production per miner in the northeast was 0.33 tons per day. It is now, in 1952, nearly double this figure. In 1949 the value of industrial production in the northeast represented 35 percent of the total industrial and agricultural production. By 1950 it had risen to 43 percent, and the target for 1951 is to increase to 47 percent.

Coal production for the entire country increased nearly one and a half times between 1947 and 1950, production of steel more than ten times, of pig iron eleven and a half times.

During the same period production of machinery had increased three times and of cement nearly four times.

11 Oil Flows in China

CHINA has oil. The description of China as "oil poor" is false. The kind of falsehood assiduously spread by the Western oil companies, which flooded China with their own oil products and planned to keep this vast land as their own fruitful market. I recollect the day when, on my return from China via the U.S.A. in 1932, I gave a lecture in New York. I told the story of our return from Tibet. Ninety *li* from Lanchow our petrol gave out. It had been a long, tiring day, culminating in improvised transport across a deep and rapid river on ferry boats precariously fashioned as car carriers. Major Todd and I had walked the whole distance through the Chinese night to get a fresh supply. At the end of the lecture, a tall, fine-looking man man approached me with a notebook: "Name the place Mr. Dean," he said, "where you could not get gas. It should never be said that there was any place on God's earth, least of all in China, where you asked in vain for Standard Oil."

Well, that day is gone, and not a hundred miles from the very spot where our "gas" supply ran out stand the oil derricks of Kansu, *China's* oil derricks. These desolate northwest expanses bid fair to become a major industrial center of China.

At the China National Petroleum Exhibition held in Peking in December, 1951, an illuminated chart showed the sources of oil throughout the country, particularly in its northwestern, southwestern, and northern and eastern provinces. A geological survey party, three times as numerous as in pre-Liberation days, was busy scouring Chinese territory for oil, with heartening results. China has now five oil regions, northern Shensi, western Kansu, central Kansu, the Hohsi corridor, and Sinkiang.

All these regions have now their own oil-refining facilities.

The output of crude oil in China in 1951 was 90 percent above the average of the last five years of the Kuomintang rule.

Manufacture of oil products also marks a peak, 50 percent higher in 1951 than in 1949. Kerosene production was 40 percent higher and the National Petroleum Corporation registered 150 percent above the previous peak. Oil processing develops. The northeast produces the high-octane gasoline used by Chinese airplanes. Oil-bearing sands also yield their quota of distilled oil.

Oil, however, is refined elsewhere than in the far west. Fushan, whose coal mine we visited, has its own synthetic gasoline plant, a thermal cracking plant to process oil-bearing minerals, a polymerization plant which produces high-quality gasoline from gas released in the cracking plant, and a high-pressure hydrogenation plant.

China's oil industry has made greater strides since the Liberation than in the whole previous half-century. The Liberation Government has released the productive forces of the country. All too long had China's rich resources been chained up, and deliberately chained up, to facilitate the influx of foreign oil. It is fifty years since the first drillings discovered oil in the Yenchang oilfields in North Shensi Province; since then little or nothing had been done to develop it. Only when the People's Army made its base there did the oil flow. And not all the Kuomintang blockade could stop that flow, though it could hinder fresh equipment from reaching the area.

The American monopolies had after V-J Day gone out of their way to stop the natural growth of the oil industry. Not until China had cast off her semi-colonial status could her oil resources yield their riches.

Liberation has sent the work forward with a bound. The thermal cracking plant in the northeast was built in four months, the synthetic gasoline plant in half a year. Efficiency has increased. The drilling machinery used is now home-made. Oil deficiency is on the decrease. China is building up her own oil industry, which will supply her own vast and ever-increasing needs.

PART III. BUILDERS OF THE NEW CHINA

1 The People's Leaders

THE successful revolution which has changed in so radical a fashion the whole course of Chinese history was not spontaneous. It had predecessors. There had been many revolutions in China before this one and as many failures. Failures due, in the main, to lack of instructed and resolute leaders knit together into a guiding party; lack, too, of an approved "know-how."

The China of the successful revolution had, in embryo, both leaders and program: potential Party leaders, some, like Chu Teh and Chou En-lai, studying in Europe and some, like Mao Tse-tung, still in China: all gradually converging and taking form in the Communist Party, formed in Shanghai, the center of China's industrial activity, on July 1, 1921.

Leaders are focal points of revolutions, and demand and reward a careful study. I confine myself to four outstanding men, though there are many more: Chou En-lai, Chu Teh, Peng Teh-huai, and Mao Tse-tung.

CHOU EN-LAI

Handsome, courteous, and gently spoken, Chou En-lai hides under a modest urbane presence a courage of steel with reasoning power swift and trenchant as a rapier. "Chou En-lai is the ablest diplomat in the world, not excepting Mr. Churchill," was Dean Acheson's estimate. And

I well remember the caustic reply that Chou En-lai once made to a wild assertion of Acheson, who, speaking pontifically, had overlooked the vast size, the huge population, and outstanding importance of this quarter of the human race to whom he was dictating: "Study the map, Mr. Acheson, and think again" were Chou's concluding words.

Reading those words and studying the part Chou En-lai had taken in the Chinese struggle and the place he now occupies as Chinese Premier and Foreign Minister, I was naturally anxious to meet him. We had met Madame Chou En-lai, his wife—a strong and competent lady—and his daughter at a long interview. She spoke for two or three hours answering our questions, skilfully outlining to my wife the place women occupy in the new China.

Our wish to see the Prime Minister was gratified. He invited us to a private family dinner and an evening of informal talk; a memorable evening and an illuminating talk.

Mr. Chou's face once seen is never forgotten. An alert and kindly face, youthful, almost boyish, set in a frame of dark hair, with dark eyes, shining beneath dark brows. A Chinese face, of course, but with unusually deep-set eyes for China. A very warmly kind face too, and with eyes that look straight at you. I cannot imagine a less aggressive face, or a gentler one. But under the charm and the calm was a complete assurance and a sense of command. After devastating an opponent with keen logic, I can well imagine him smiling with the same kindly and benign though slightly sarcastic look as his opponent gathered himself together and licked his wounds. Such a look he surely had when he said: "Study the map, Mr. Acheson, and think again."

Chou is an intellectual. He is cultivated. He looks what he is, the scion of a great Mandarin family, his father famous as a teacher, his mother as a reader of modern literature. He himself has all the elements of literary genius. But what was difficult to imagine, as one sat with him at dinner and in the drawing room afterward with all the culture of ancient China around him, all the unostentatious, exquisite taste of the rooms and the chaste simplicity of his dress—fawn-colored trousers, well-creased, and fawn-colored tunic buttoned high up, without collar or tie, to the neck—was this same man preparing in his youthful days an insurrection, helping the National Army to seize Shanghai; this gentle man stimulating 600,000 workers in a militant strike—to imagine him as a leader of the Third Revolution that raised the Red Banner in China, or as a leader in the 7,000-mile Long March; as a man whose courage, tenacity, and resolute action made perfect balance with his wide knowledge and cultured intelligence.

The even tenor of Chou En-lai's promising childhood, with its cultured tastes and literary beauty, was rudely disturbed by the great national awakening of the First Revolution of 1911. The thoughtful lad was caught up in the current of China's new birth. Outstanding as a student in the American-backed missionary Nankai Middle School and then in Nankai University in Tientsin, he had paid his own way by scholarships. In the student rebellion of 1919, as a student leader in the struggle for democracy and as one of the founders of the "Awakening Society" which led the organization of radical youth, Chou was arrested and imprisoned for a year. A radical girl student, Miss Teng Ying-ch'ao, jailed at the same time and for the same offense, became his wife. It was hard as we sat in the cultured seclusion of the Chou dinner party, with wife and daughter as perfect hostesses, to picture the young Chou and the young girl—she must have been, at the period of their imprisonment, as young and charming as the daughter is now—in the tumult of student strife, and suffering the shame of a Chinese jail.

But the conviction which brought them to arrest and imprisonment ran deep and has carried them far. On his release, Chou went to France, as Chu Teh had gone to Germany, to learn more of communism and to help to organize the Chinese Communist Party in Paris. Study in France and Germany; a short stay in England; and in three years' time, in 1924, Chou returned to China, a revolutionary organizer who joined up with Sun Yat-sen, who was at that time preparing for the Nationalist Revolution in Canton. His advance was rapid. At the age of twenty-six he became Secretary of the Whampoa Military Academy, working in intimate connection with General Bluecher, who ultimately became Commander of the Soviet Far Eastern Army.

Chiang Kai-shek, as Commander-in-Chief of the new Nationalist Army of China, elected to that office jointly by the Kuomintang and the Communists, who at this time worked in uneasy unity in China's Nationalist Front, was engaged during 1925-27 on his Northern Expedition. He ordered Chou En-lai, whom he cordially disliked, but whose hold on the cadets made him indispensable, to raise revolt in Shanghai. Within three months this young student of twenty-eight, with no military training and scarcely any knowledge of the working class save that born of deep sympathy with them, organized a strike of 600,000 workers in the greatest and most imperialistically dominated city of the East, under the frowning guns of battle-gray foreign warships. The strike was not followed by revolt. It was easily crushed. The workers had no armed nucleus.

Chou and his comrades remedied this. They organized 50,000 pickets and secretly trained 2,000 cadres. Armed revolt broke out on May 21, 1927, with 600,000 workers on strike. The police-station arsenal and garrison were captured and a "Citizen Government" proclaimed. When Chiang Kai-shek arrived, he found the city subdued and the Communist force triumphant. A month later Chiang Kai-shek attacked the very men who had won the victory for him. Chou's name was first on the list of the proscribed.

Chou fled from the Kuomintang and raised the Red Standard at Nanchang. But not before dozens of his close companions had been executed—5,000 was the estimate of deaths in the "Shanghai Massacre."

Chou himself was captured. He only escaped death by the influence of an old fellow student of his Whampoa Academy days.

Under Chou En-lai the workers seized the seaport of Swatow and held it for ten days against foreign and native forces. Under Chou En-lai they organized the Canton Commune.

With the defeat of Canton, Chou hid until he could escape in 1931 to Kiangsi and Fukien, where he became political commissar to Chu Teh, the Commander-in-Chief of the Red Army, also, but later, becoming Vice-Chairman of the Revolutionary Military Council.

On the collapse of the small gallant revolutionary base of the South, in face of overwhelming force, Chou En-lai fought his way out of the new base in the far northwest.

Neither Chou En-lai nor Chu Teh was of peasant or workingclass origin, no more than was Karl Marx or Lenin, but, like them, none was more devoted to the working masses and none more deeply convinced that only through the working masses could the revolution triumph.

CHU TEH

Chu Teh's career is probably the most romantic of the four. Chu Teh's is the case of a man converted to a cause in middle life, and so thoroughly converted that at forty years of age he forsook not only wealth and prestige and all the luxury which that meant in the old China, but broke a life-long vicious habit as an opium-smoker, and then endured as leader of a poverty-stricken, bitterly-assailed army the untold hardships of a soldier's life in the most memorable and hazardous march in history, through scorching heat and bitter cold, emerging at long length as Commander-in-Chief of the most triumphant army the Far East has ever seen.

Born into a landlord's family, Chu Teh inherited power and wealth. He drifted down, while still a youth, through a life of luxury and self-indulgence into a soul-destroying dissipation.

Chu Teh had nine wives and several concubines. From early years he had been an opium-smoker. But in his youth he had generous instincts and had been stimulated by the ancient heroic legends of his race. Naturally, under such stimulus the boy chose a military life and received a modern Western military training at the Yunnan Academy, playing a leading part subsequently in the overthrow of the Manchu Dynasty in 1912. This established his prestige. He rose rapidly to high positions. But he fell just as rapidly into the prevailing vices of high officialdom, opium-smoking, battening on political funds to purchase a palatial dwelling for his wives and concubines.

Deep down, however, and beneath all this surface rottenness there smoldered the fires of the old idealism and revolutionary feeling. He found himself surrounded in Yunnan with thousands of slave boys and girls. What of them? The Revolution of 1911 had proved abortive as far as these young creatures and the common people were concerned. This so-called revolution was not modernizing China.

Chu Teh was seriously disturbed. He was anxious and curious to know more about the liberal movements of the West. He read. He studied. He traveled. Something in him exploded. Pensioning off his wives and concubines, he went to Shanghai, sought out the most revolutionary spirits of the Kuomintang, which he had joined. Stimulated by his new friends, he made a desperate effort to break the opium habit, lying on his bed for a week almost unconscious in the struggle to conquer his craving, subsequently traveling for a month on a Yangtze steamer, where he could neither buy nor smoke opium. His will triumphed. He conquered.

Chu Teh was now forty and strong. He entered a new life. Traveling with Chinese students to Germany, he began a course of reading which led him to Marxism. He joined, in Hanover, the Chinese Branch of the Communist Party.

Chu Teh, according to Commander Li Chiang-lin, had an experienced, disciplined, practical mind. He lived the simple life of a soldier. He had joined the Communist Party influenced by the same motives that had made him, at an early age, join the Kuomintang—sympathy for the poor. Now he cordially agreed with Sun Yat-sen's "land to the tiller" policy and limitation of private capitalism. Further knowledge of Marxism had, however, begun to reveal the inadequacy of Sun Yat-sen's program, and Chu advanced to more radical ideas.

Urged on by the Chinese Communist students, he went to Moscow and studied Marxism. Thence he returned to Shanghai. He gave his fortune to the Communist Party and worked under their direction at his post in the Kuomintang and on the staff of General Chu Pei-teh, second in command to Chiang Kai-shek.

On August 1, 1927, Chu Pei-Teh bade him crush the Communist insurrectionists. He refused. Coming out openly as a Communist, he revolted and, together with his police and the regiment he was training, marched south and, with part of the Ninth Army, after taking Swatow, he withdrew to Kiangsi and Hunan. Retreating to Fukien later with a force that had dwindled to 900 men and 500 rifles, he joined up with General Fan Shih-sheng, who was tolerating Communists in his army that he might use them as tools against Chiang Kai-shek, whom he hated.

Fan's army was not all of one mind concerning the Communists, and an anti-Communist section planned an attack on Chu Teh's life. Surrounding the inn where he was staying, in the semi-dark they seized him and aimed revolvers at his head. "Don't shoot me," he cried. "I'm only the cook. Don't shoot a man who can cook for you."

Pausing, they hauled him outside into the light. A man recognized him and cried out, "Here is Chu Teh! Kill him!" Quick as lightning, Chu Teh, pulling out his own revolver, shot the informer dead. Then, overpowering the guard, he escaped. Ever since then he has been popularly known in the Army as "Chief Cook."

In financial extremities, and with a dwindling force, Chu Teh divided his army, scantily fed and clad almost in rags, into three sections, allocating to each its special task and calling the whole "The Peasants' Army." Controlling a district on the Hunan-Kiangsi-Kwangtung border and beginning there a program of tax abolition, redistribution of land, and confiscation of the property of the rich, he was at length approached by Mao Tse-tung, who, likewise hard-pressed, had seized the well-nigh impregnable hilltop sanctuary of Chingkang on the South Kiangsi-Hunan border with instructions from the Communist Party that he and Chu Teh should join forces and operate a program of partisan warfare, agrarian reconstruction, and the building of socialism. The two armies joined in May, 1928, 50,000 strong, with 4,000 rifles, together with unarmed party workers and the army men's families.

The next six years were critical in China's history. Mao Tse-tung welded the Red Army into a highly-instructed and disciplined force and launched it on its terrific march of 7,000 miles. Chu Teh had defeated every general sent against him, though fighting always against terrible odds, against forces sometimes eight, nine, or even more times the size of his own forces. His tactical ingenuity, mobility, versatility, and courage had always triumphed, and he had emerged at length as the military leader of China. If in the south the Red Army had suffered from strategic mistakes due to political blunders, after the Long March it emerged triumphant, thanks to Chu Teh's genius for generalship and to the devotion of himself and his men to a cause which he not only espoused, but inspired.

Chu Teh's Liberation Army men were devoted to him because he was devoted to them. He dressed like them and lived like them, sharing their hardships and their pleasures. He could be stern as a schoolmaster and ruthless as a surgeon, but through it all there was with him, as with Mao Tse-tung and Chou En-lai and Peng Teh-huai a passionate desire for a free and prosperous China, the benefits of which all alike could share.

PENG TEH-HUAI

Peng Teh-huai joined Mao Tse-tung at Chingkang when the Communist forces were in process of preparation for their great tasks and the Long March. This broad-shouldered, stocky, cheerful, smiling general did much to form the character of the Eighth Route Army in the later days of the revolutionary struggle.

Peng, whose home was not far from that of Mao Tse-tung, neither smoked nor drank. He slept little and rose early. He could outstrip most of the younger men at climbing or other feats. Like his brother generals, he never spared himself. He walked on foot most of the 7,000 miles of the Long March, lending his horse to tired and wounded comrades.

Peng's Eighth Route Army was as frugal as himself. The whole Army of 40,000 men could be kept for long on the price of the reward set on his own head, dead or alive. Yet so beloved was the man that he wandered fearlessly in town or countryside without any bodyguard and with only one sentry at night standing in front of his home. Peng's Red Army was the People's Army. He was one with the people and the Army alike. Hence he knew no fear and had no fear.

Peng was peculiarly fond of children. He was often to be seen surrounded by buglerboys, messboys, orderlies, or groomboys—"Little Red Devils" they were called—earnestly talking with them of their troubles or of public affairs. He took them seriously.

Perhaps his sympathies went out to boys because his own boyhood had been unhappy. Unhappy at home, with a jealous stepmother and a still more cruel grandmother, he was also unhappy at school, where goaded one day by cruel beatings, he had retaliated by flinging a stool at his master. This led to a lawsuit and his stepmother renouncing him. Let Edgar Snow repeat the rest of the tale of his home life:

"My grandmother regarded us all as her slaves. She was a heavy smoker of opium. I hated the smell of it, and one night, when I could stand it no longer, I got up and kicked a pan of her opium from the stove. She was furious, called a meeting of the whole clan and demanded my death by drowning."

The clan agreed. His own mother's brother, however, saved him from death. But at nine years of age he was turned adrift, taking now this job, now that. At sixteen he joined his uncle because he was betrothed to his cousin. But when he attached himself to the starving peasants during the rice famine and, storming a rich man's house, compelled the rich man to sell his rice without profit, he had to flee. He joined Sun Yat-sen's revolutionary army, himself a rebel. Captured at Changsha, he was tortured for a month in the cells before release. Re-enlisting, he became a battalion commander.

A reader like Mao and Chu Teh, he moved continually to the left. On reading *The Communist Manifesto,* he began to work with conviction for the new society. His own description of the origin and growth of the Red Army is excellent: "Arising from rural bankruptcy, the fruit of imperialism, landlordism and militaristic wars, the poverty-stricken peasants were ripe for revolt. The hinterlands of China, bridgeless, road-less and rail-less, fostered the growth of the Partisans. The imperialists, bitterly opposed to the Partisans, lacked cohesion." More will be said later of China's partisan warfare and of Peng's description of it.

MAO TSE-TUNG

We drank tea on a lovely summer afternoon in June with Chairman Mao Tse-tung—he is always referred to as "Chairman Mao"—in a large cool Chinese room at the Winter Palace in Peking. A room as Chinese as Chinese could be. Artistically, China at its best. Exquisite in taste and simplicity. Not Dowager Empress China, cluttered with nineteenth century Birmingham bric-a-brac, locomotive clocks, and weather-glass steamers or mechanical birds that flap wings and whistle.

No, just Chinese; quiet and sedate, rich, blue-carpeted floors, scroll wall-paintings, lacquered door-screens, and lattice windows opening onto wide-flagged courtyards, formal with flower-pots and goldfish tubs. An ancient palace building, ground floor only, as, happily, is general in Peking, its golden-tiled roof as new as if finished yesterday, its up-turned, glittering cornice in golden and vivid contrast to the blue sky.

Chou En-lai, the Premier, greeted us. Tea was brought. Mao Tse-tung came in. The same Mao whose portrait is seen and revered from one end of China to the other, revered by a quarter of the human race. Rather older than the portrait, but the same strong head, held well back on powerful shoulders. A big man, if not tall.

But it was neither the size nor the strength that arrested our attention. Nor even the signs of suffering—he had lost his dearly beloved wife on the Long March and had seen many of his best friends fall at his side; he had seen poverty, misery, and death. All that too had left its mark upon his face. But what struck us most was something no picture had ever caught, an inexpressible look of kindness and sympathy, an obvious preoccupation with the needs of others: other people's difficulties, other people's troubles, other people's struggles—these formed the deep content of his thoughts and needed but a touch or a word to bring this unique look of sympathy to his face.

I mentioned the floods of 1932, when last I was in China. A sudden shadow overcast him as he mentally pictured that flood, the famine which followed it, the agonizing looks of famished parents watching their starving children die. Slowly he said: "They were not organized then." The words and the look gave a clue to Mao's character: intense compassion for China's common suffering folk, intense belief too that their suffering could be ended if they were *organized.*

It was not hard as you talked with Chairman Mao to understand the deep affection men feel for this man who has organized life on a human basis for hundreds of millions of Chinese men and women. All men—intellectuals, peasants, merchants—regard Mao as the symbol of their deliverance, the man who shared their troubles and has raised their burdens. The peasant looks at the land he tills: Mao's gift. The factory worker thinks of a wage of 100 pounds of rice instead of 10: Mao's gift. The intellectual, rejoicing in freedom from the menace of armed censorship, regards that too as Mao's gift.

It was Mao and his band of inspired comrades who, living with the people, suffering with the people, and working with the people, had led the people on from conquest to conquest; who had reorganized army strategy; who had welded the army into a victorious force; who had given land to the peasants, liberty to womanhood, and the gifts of the mastery of rivers, floods, and drought to all; who had conquered graft, dishonesty, and all other forms of corrupt administration. It was Mao who had inspired men to band together and work in teams.

By good fortune, I had on a previous visit come to know Mao's home town of Changsha. I visited Changsha in 1932. I visited it again in 1952, marveling at the change since the Liberation. The dirty, decrepit shacks running far along the river front are gone, replaced by a promenade. The 12,000-ton heap of centuries-old filth has gone, removed by voluntary labor. A newly-constructed highway—with huge main drainpipes, ready to solve Changsha's sewage problem—already near completion, runs from station to riverside.

Other changes, too, reveal the change in political life. No British warships patrol the river now, no American guns dominate the town from a fort on the island. Ditches are dried and cleaned. Buses replace rickshaws. A steam ferry transports 6,000 people daily across the river, and far away a huge reservoir will soon provide this city of a quarter of a million people with a pure and uncontaminated water supply.

Some things in Changsha happily remain unchanged, some things which still speak of the days when Mao Tse-tung was a lad, a teacher, an organizer, and a lecturer there. As, for example, that small barn-like lecture hall, fitted with rough desks and benches, a raised dais for a presiding lecturer at one end, set under a portrait of an old Chinese scholar looking dignified in his tall hat; the walls hung with texts from the old Chinese classics.

In that hall Mao Tse-tung had run an institute from 1921 to 1923, after his years of schooling, after his visits to Peking, and after he had become a Communist.

There, too, is the Normal School to which he went as a pupil and to which later he returned as a teacher.

I heard many tales here of Mao Tse-tung's struggles with reactionary rulers, of his instructions to students and of his championing of the workers' cause. I learned much from an old fellow pupil who still lives and works at Changsha. That early story has been enlarged by Mao himself and told at length in Edgar Snow's admirable book, *Red Star Over China,* now unhappily out of print; but the old fellow pupil had his own additions to make. He grew lyrical as he told of the early morning when Mao had mustered the students and had led them to attack the slumbering soldiers of the hated general in command of the city, to seize their weapons and force the general to retreat.

Mao's own story starts earlier. Born at Shao Shan, 150 *li* from Changsha, Mao was one of a family of five. His father was a poor peasant, who climbed by industry into the middle peasant class, and then to the rich peasant class. Debt had driven him into the Army. On his release he saved and rebought his 15 *mou* of land, which raised an annual 60 *piculs* of rice. The family of five each consumed 7 *piculs,* leaving 25 *piculs,* with which in time Mao senior bought 7 more *mou* of land and became a rich peasant. By industry he became a trader in beans. A stern man, he always made his children work hard: Mao was bred and reared in a tough school.

Mao began farming when six years of age, working early morning and late at night, right through his five years at primary school, from the age of eight to thirteen. His teacher, like his father, was a stern man, and fond of the cane. At ten the boy ran away from home and wandered for three days. When found by his parents, he was taken home and received milder treatment. "My first strike," he said, "was successful!"

His father made Mao keep the family accounts at night, gave him no money and little food, not even the one egg with rice which he gave on the fifteenth of each month to the laborer. Mao never ate meat.

His father, fond of moralizing, had the habit of quoting the classics to the boy, as an English parent might quote Scripture: "Boys must work and not be lazy." The lad was resilient. He retorted, also from the classics: "Older people do more work than the young; you are three times my age; you should work three times as hard."

A climax came one day when his father had shamed him before a party of friends. He ran out of the house and, when pursued, stood on the brink of a pond, threatening to drown himself if they touched him.

Argument followed; demand and counter-demand. He had won, though he consented to return and give a partial *kou-tou* to his father. Another lesson learned, he said: "Rebellion won victory"—through weak submission formerly, his father had beaten and crushed him the more.

So the lad grew. His strong dislike of his father, who was militantly anti-religious—his mother being a devout Buddist—also grew, and had at least one good consequence: it drove him to hard and thorough work at the family bookkeeping, to give his father no cause for blows; and also at the Classics, which he personally disliked, to save trouble at school and provide quotations in debate.

The romances of old China were his real love, especially the tales of rebellion.

At thirteen he left school. He worked full time for his father on the farm. At night he continued at his father's books. Later still at night—blocking the light of his window with a curtain—he read all he could find of other books more to his own liking, books like *Words of Warning* by an old reformist scholar, who urged that China was weak because she had no Western appliances—railways, telegraphs, and the like. Reading made him skeptical. He was seeking for richer moral fare. It also fired him to continue his studies. He sought further schooling. His father refused to hear of it.

So again Mao ran away and studied for half a year with a friend. While there he saw one day the bean merchants fleeing from Changsha. There had been a famine. Thousands were starving. Appeals to the governor had brought the retort: "Why haven't you food? There is plenty in the city. I always have enough." The people came out in the streets and drove the governor away. A new governor provided help, but was removed, as the emperor disliked his "connection with the mob." The man who succeeded him forthwith arrested and beheaded the leaders of the revolt. Mao was deeply moved. He felt that the rebels were ordinary people like his own family. The injustice rankled with the lad.

From this time onward, throughout his school years, Mao groped his way to advanced social and political thought. His active, rebellious, and explorative mind was not easily satisfied. In choice of school he was curiously fastidious and by no means afraid of changing his mind. At the age of sixteen he started at a new school, recommended by a cousin, where less attention was paid to the Classics and more to Western knowledge, a school based on more radical educational methods; he spent six months there. Then he left. He had made good progress, and it was cheap. It was also snobbish. His clothes were old. He was not a "native." He felt humiliated, frozen, and depressed. He applied for admission to the big Middle School at Changsha and was accepted on the strength of an ably-written essay. He stayed there six months and joined the Army after reading of the Canton uprising against the Manchus, and after he had learned about Sun Yat-sen and his program. The anti-foreign movement against the construction of the Szechuan-Hankow Railway by foreign capitalists, and the refusal of demands for a Parliament, had agitated and stung the students, who cut off their "Manchu" pigtails. In the Army Mao had learned more of socialism and social reform. After half a year, he "returned to the books."

New schools of various kinds were founded in those unsettled times and vied with one another in advertisement. Mao studied the advertisements and, deciding on a police school, paid the dollar admission fee. A soapmakers' school, stressing the social benefits of soap, changed his mind. He invested another dollar on another entrance fee. Then came a succession of changes at a dollar apiece—law school, commercial school, higher commercial school. Finally, he found a temporary anchor in the First Provincial Middle School. After that he left school altogether and began to study on his own account.

Mao's schedule for his home study was severe. With only a rice cake for dinner, he spent every moment in the Hunan Provincial Library, reading from opening to closing time. He considered this the most valuable period of his educational life. He read widely and avidly—world geography, world history, Adam Smith's *Wealth of Nations,* Darwin's *Origin of Species,* John Stuart Mill, Rousseau, Herbert Spencer.

Pressed by his father to decide on a career, Mao chose to be a teacher, and after five years of study—his parents consenting—at the Hunan Normal School, with cheap board and lodgings and no tuition fees, he got his degree.

Mao had desired serious friends. He had advertised for companions, for youths disciplined in character, determined and ready to make sacrifices for their country. The first three who answered were failures, but with other and better men he built up a serious-minded group. They talked of large matters—"The nature of man, of human society, of China, the world and the Universe!"

During these later school years Mao built up a wide correspondence, which led in 1907 to a more closely-knit organization called "The New People's Society" with seventy or eighty members—names subsequently to become famous in the Chinese communist movement.

Mao's bill of expenses while at the Normal School makes interesting reading: extraordinary in its moderation: only $160 for five years; extraordinary too in its composition: one-third spent on newspapers, books, and journals. His father "cursed" him for his extravagance. Newspapers were novelties and shunned by the official mind. Mao was, however, an eager student and determined to be well informed.

After school, Mao went to Peking, where he helped to organize the movement by which young students went to France to study under the "work and earn" scheme through which France had recruited young Chinese workers to her cause during the 1914-18 war. Many students from the Hunan Normal School went to France and returned to become famous.

Mao, needing money, got work as sublibrarian at Peking University Library—a lowly job, with many indignities. But with compensations too. For here he met and fell in love with Yang Kai-jui, daughter of his former ethics teacher—the teacher who had made a great impression upon him in his youth. Later he married Miss Yang.

Mao was always a serious student. Far back in his schooldays he had lived an earnest and austere life. At Changsha, in the school grounds where Mao had studied, the old fellow revolutionary to whom I have referred spoke much of Mao's stern, self-disciplined life at school. He showed us the well where Mao used to wash himself in the open, even in wintertime. He told us how Mao sought exact knowledge of distant regions. And how, to this latter end, and stimulated by the experience of two fellow students who went to Tibet, Mao had walked with a friend through five counties, visiting the Tung Ting Lake, sleeping at peasant homes and writing peasants' letters in return for his board. His tour had cost him not a copper.

As a scholar Mao was thorough. There still exists a book of 100,000 words with Mao's annotations in it. The annotations run to 20,000 words. As a student he was much influenced by a young teacher, but lately returned from England, Yang Chen-chi by name, who was an idealist and urged him to be just, moral, virtuous, and useful. Mao and his serious friends ordered their lives by rule: (1) Not to talk of trivial things, (2) Not to talk of money. (3) Not to talk of sex.

Mao's poverty led to hardship, in overcrowded lodgings—seven in a tiny room—with scarcely air to breathe. But he was fascinated, as we were, with the parks and the old palace grounds, and with Peking's innumerable trees; fascinated with the early northern spring, where the white plum blossoms flowered while ice held solid the northern sea; fascinated with the willow trees dangling with ice crystals glittering in the winter sunlight.

His tour in the north left many a deep impression with him: ice on the Gulf of Pei Hai, the walk on Nanking's Wall, the climb up Cai Shan, the visit to Confucius' grave. His tour had also made a deep impression

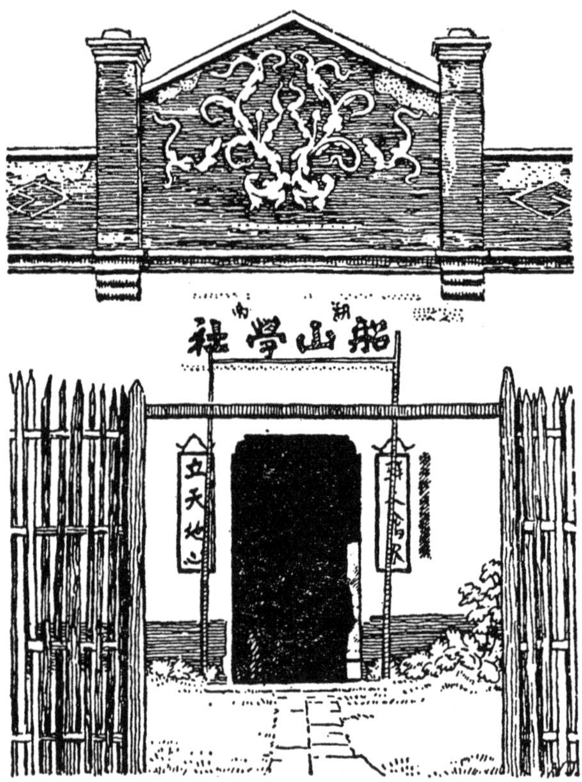

In that simple hall Mao Tse-tung ran revolutionary classes from 1921 to 1923.

on his mind politically and socially. He returned to Changsha with the determination to take a more direct role in politics. He became editor of the *Hsiang Chiang Review,* the Hunan student paper, which exercised great influence on the student movement in South China. He founded and aided various societies. He organized students. He organized workers.

In May, 1921, Mao attended the foundation meeting of the Communist Party in Shanghai.

Simultaneously a Chinese Communist Party was formed in France by worker-students there, among them, as we saw on an earlier page, Chou En-lai, and shortly afterward in Germany with Chu Teh among its first members.

This leads us inevitably to the story of the Chinese Communist Party, where all these various vigorous minds set themselves to work in unison for the regeneration of China upon socialist and communist lines, as set forth by Marx and Lenin.

2 Party and Army

THE FIRST REVOLUTIONARY CIVIL WAR

So inseparably interwoven are the stories of the Communist Party and the Red Army that they must here be treated together. I had planned to treat each in isolation. The task was impracticable.

The pressure that drove China to revolution came at the right time. It came when the Russian Revolution of 1917 was providing a model and filling men's minds with new hope. At a time, too, when the political situation in China was ripe for drastic change. The successful revolution in Russia, based on the teachings of Marx, supplied the program.

Furthermore, the economic and political situation in the China of 1921 was no less favorable for change. Western capitalism, invading China, had given rise to modern industry—small indeed in bulk in proportion to population and strictly controlled by Western industrialists to keep intact the colonial status of China, but not so insignificant that it left China with no industrial working class nucleus. Chinese industry had given rise to a proletariat resentful against ruthless profit-making capitalism and anti-national imperialism, the nucleus of a class which could enlist under its banner all working people. Elements for the struggle were assembled.

Further again, Western capitalism, though it came with its own fetters, had the effect of hastening Chinese feudalism to its final collapse.

For China's feudal landlords and warlords had found in Western imperialistic capitalism a useful ally, with whose help they temporarily strengthened their hold on the peasantry. It was a precarious security, encouraging insolence, brutality, and greed. Peasant poverty and with it elements of agrarian revolt increased apace. All that was needed was resolute and instructed leadership.

It was in this situation that the Chinese Communist Party was launched at Shanghai by fifty resolute men acting through their twelve delegates. The Party, born thirty years ago, has led the Chinese people through four exceedingly difficult revolutionary wars:

1. The First Revolutionary Civil War, 1925-27.
2. The Second Revolutionary Civil War, 1927-36.
3. The War of Resistance to Japan, 1937-45.
4. The Third Revolutionary Civil War and the Foundation of the People's Republic of China, 1945-49.

It emerged immensely strong and now leads over a quarter of the human race.

Growing rapidly in strength and numbers after its foundation in 1921, the Communist Party slowly felt its way in the struggle for the people's cause. At its second Party Congress in 1922 it issued a manifesto, which laid down as basic tasks the overthrow of the warlords, resistance to international imperialism, Chinese independence, and Chinese unity.

So far so good, but lacking in two further fundamental steps: proletarian leadership of the revolution and political power to back the peasants' demand for land.

The tide of struggle grew. More than 300,000 workers participated in 100 strikes in major cities. Reactionary resistance also grew and in the railway strike of 1923 forty workers were killed and many hundreds wounded in what came later to be known as the "February 7th Massacre" of Hankow. The lesson was obvious and quickly learned: without strong allies and its own armed forces, the Chinese working class could not defeat the reactionaries in a land where the people had no democratic rights.

Seeking allies, the Party united with Dr. Sun's Kuomintang, a body formed to carry on the bourgeois-democratic struggle, after the Revolution of 1911, which had overthrown the Peking warlords, had collapsed. Giving active support to Dr. Sun, the Party helped to organize the revolutionary Military Academy in Whampoa and the Kuomintang troops.

At this critical moment in January, 1925, Dr. Sun Yat-sen died.

The nation expressed its grief by widespread political propaganda and by a big strike in May against British and Japanese industrialists in Shanghai, following the killing of a Communist worker by a Japanese mill owner. British police fired on the demonstrators. British and Japanese goods were boycotted. Hong Kong was blockaded. The whole nation demanded redress.

This "May 30th Movement" paved the way for countrywide revolution. The Communist Party was in the forefront of activity. Kwangtung Province was rapidly unified. Its National Revolutionary Army set out in July, 1926, on the Northern Expedition. Quickly defeating the reactionary warlords, it occupied Hankow. Shanghai also rose. Trade union membership reached 2,800,000; Peasants Associations, 9,500,000. The membership of the Communist Party rose from 900 to 57,000.

Unfortunately, all this enthusiasm lacked its own people's military force and leadership. Chen Tu-hsiu, leader at that time of the Communist Party in the Kuomintang Government, had no love for proletarian leadership. He gave no support to the mass movement demanding land. He took no steps to create the masses' own armed forces. Communist soldiers fought in the Kuomintang Army, but actual power, even in the Northern Expeditionary Army, was still in the hands of old-type officers. Chiang Kai-shek was commander-in-chief of the "National Revolutionary Army." He yielded, not unwillingly, to the landlord and bourgeois elements, who hated mass movements. They proceeded to attack the Communist Party. The Party for the moment could put up no effective resistance. The First Revolutionary War had failed.

SECOND REVOLUTIONARY CIVIL WAR

But the Communist Party was by no means overwhelmed. Persecution mounted to massacre. To be a Communist was a crime punishable by death. "The Kuomintang would rather kill a thousand in error than have one Communist escape."* But the Communist Party fought on. They "were not frightened, not conquered, not annihilated. They stood up again, wiped off the bloodstains and went on fighting."

On August 1, 1927, when the Party headed the Nanchang uprising, with Chou En-lai leading 30,000 men southward to the Kwangtung Province, the Red Army was born and from that moment onward worked as an independent force. Chiang Kai-shek might have gained control of the cities. He had lost control of the rural areas. He had moved from the people. Numerically, his army was strong. Numerically, the Communist Party was weak. The Communist Party and its Army, however, based on the people, were potentially strong.

The leadership of the Chinese Revolution had now passed from the Kuomintang Government at Wuhan to the Communist Party and its army. Chiang Kai-shek led a vigorous counter-revolutionary movement. Aiming at virtual dictatorship, he disbanded the Kuomintang Government at Wuhan and formed at Nanking a government more amenable to himself, continuing with even less hindrance than before his savage attacks on the Communist Party.

The Party itself, now thrown on its own resources, acted drastically. It removed Chen, the traitor Secretary. It launched Autumn Harvest Uprisings in several places in 1927; ultimately, though not at first, it gave up the struggle in the cities and redoubled the struggle in the rural districts, led in this policy primarily by Mao, who had seized a strong position in the most inaccessible mountain of Chingkang and there was busily building up revolutionary troops, workers, pickets, and peasants into a real workers' and peasants' Red Army. Mao also began to distribute land to the landless peasants.

This point was crucial in Communist Party activities. Here was the opportunity for which Mao Tse-tung had longed. Here he could put into practice the policy, by which alone China could triumph, of mobilizing China's 300 million peasant population, protecting them, and satisfying their age-long land hunger.

* That was the situation and a common saying when I was in China in 1932. I saw a man shot before my eyes in Hangchow: "a suspected Communist." And I saw the 350,000 refugee workers on dyke reparation east of Hankow disbanded at a fortnight's notice by the Kuomintang general, despite the protests of the American Bishop Rootes and the New Zealander Rewi Alley, who were in charge of the International Famine Relief Fund, which was organizing refugee work: "There are Communists among them: if they are not gone in two weeks I shall turn machine guns on them." They were driven away and their shelters destroyed and 40 percent of the grain donated for refugee relief found its way to the warlords' "go-downs."

Mao was precisely the man to see the need and act on what he saw. Mao was of peasant stock. He was no city man. He was a countryman. He knew the hunger of a peasant: hunger for food, and hunger for land on which he could grow the food. He knew peasant problems and the peasants' stubborn determination. He visualized the overwhelming numbers of Chinese peasantry: hundreds of millions of them. He knew that without peasants' aid no revolution could succeed. He knew that with their aid, with arms in their hands and hope in their hearts, any true revolution was bound to win. Therefore he had demanded that peasants be enlisted, that peasants be armed. To urge this point, Mao wrote the most important book of this period—*Report on an Investigation into the Peasant Movement in Hunan.*

And that was just what the imperialists, the landlords, the compradores, and the upper bourgeoisie generally, together with the big men in the Kuomintang, dreaded most of all. Chen attacked Mao in the Kuomintang. He attacked Mao in the Party. But Mao had truth on his side, and now in this mountain fortress he was able to build up the peasants' and workers' army, later to be joined, as we saw, by Chu Teh.

Communist control in the south grew rapidly. The Red Army had increased to 60,000 or 70,000 by 1930. Chiang Kai-shek grew fearful and launched attack after attack. The Red Army grew to 300,000. Chiang flung a fifth attack of one million men against it in 1933. He only succeeded in defeating it when the Red Army ignored its usual Mao-planned, mobile warfare. All that was left of the Red Army broke through and joined Mao at the Chingkang mountain.

In October, 1933, Mao and Chu Teh, with all the Communist forces, began the Long March of some 7,000 miles in order to join the large Communist forces in the impregnable mountains of Shensi and Shansi, in the far northwest.

Mao took over the leadership of the whole Communist Party, of its policy, and of the strategy and tactics of the army. Through his persistent intervention and counsel, the whole peasant population was ultimately swept into the revolutionary movement. Mao and his peasant soldier army now faced the ordeal of the Long March: an outstanding military achievement which would demand a whole book to describe it. Alas, space forbids that here, and the story must only briefly be told.

THE EPIC MARCH

Nineteen hundred and thirty-four, the year of the Long March, is an epic year for China. Chiang Kai-shek's million men had broken the resistance of the Red Army in Kiangsi. In face of the growing and overwhelming numerical superiority of Chiang's forces, in face, too, of the changing political situation, following Japan's invasion of Manchuria and Shanghai, the Central Government of the Revolutionary Bases decided that the Red Army must go north, in order that all Chinese forces might combine in the Anti-Japanese War of Resistance. An appeal was issued that the Revolutionary Government was willing to co-operate with any armed forces, on the basis of cessation of civil war and of attacks on the revolutionary bases and the Red Army, with the guarantee of civil liberation and democratic rights to the masses and arming of the people for an anti-Japanese war. When it was rejected, preparations were made for the Long March.

The year 1933 had been marked by perpetual fighting, with great losses on both sides, Chiang Kai-shek had not achieved his main objective, which was to annihilate the Red Army, and now that army was preparing to slip through his fingers and he did not know it. Preparations for departure were conducted with skilled secrecy and with a retreat so swift and silent that the main force of 90,000 men had been marching several days before Chiang's headquarters knew what was happening. Regular troops had been replaced in the dead of night by partisans and the order given for the Great March, which began on October 16, 1934.

The route covered some 7,000 miles, the time one year, the terrain appalling, the problems stupendous, and the suffering sufficient to kill and break any army but one inspired through all ranks with the sense of the righteousness of its cause and with the consciousness of the immensity and gravity to China and the world of the issues involved.

In calm, unemotional words, Mao briefly summed it up in the biographical sketch which he gave to Mr. Edgar Snow, from whom again I venture to quote:

"By January, 1935, the main forces of the Red Army reached Tsun Yi, in Kweichow. For the next four months the army was almost constantly moving and the most energetic combat and fighting took place. Through many, many difficulties, across the longest and deepest and most dangerous rivers of China, across some of its highest and most hazardous mountain passes, through the country of fierce aborigines, through the empty grasslands, through cold and then intense heat, through wind and snow and rainstorm, pursued by half the White armies of

China, through all those natural barriers, and fighting its way past the local troops of Kwangtung, Hunan, Kwangsi, Kweichow, Yunan, Sikong, Szechuan, Kansu, Shensi, the Red Army reached Northern Shensi in October, 1935, and enlarged the present base in China's great northwest."

Only one or two incidents in that historic march can be hinted at here. They shall be of rivers, alps, and lonely grasslands.

The swift-flowing Yangtze surging through its deep gorges, all its boats burned by Chiang Kai-shek's order, presented an almost insuperable obstacle, only overcome by an incredible march of eighty-five miles in a single day and night for a surprise attack, and by swimming the broad, swift river to secure some boats which had escaped the burning. It was a skilled maneuver in which the entire army was transported across the Yangtze without loss of a single life.

The Tatu River, again, was an even greater problem. Chiang's forces, racing to the north bank to check the Red Army, felt, and not without reason, that they could readily annihilate the Red Army here. Again, however, by forced marches the Red Army reached the main crossing first, having traversed through the hostile Lolo country of impenetrable forests and fierce aborigines. It had been confidently supposed that this passage would absorb much time through harassing attacks. It was not so. Mao released some Lolo chiefs from Chinese prisons, treated them well, and took them home. They made the transit smooth and the river was speedily reached. Volunteers swam across and returned with boats, too few, however, to transport the army before the floods had made the passage impossible.

The only other crossing was a suspension bridge across a gorge 400 *li* higher up the river. A night-and-day race began; Chiang's troops on the northern bank, the vanguard of the Red Army on the south. Neck and neck they ran till near the bridge. Then the Red Army men drew ahead. They found that the bulk of the roadway carried by sixteen massive iron chains, was already torn away. The chains hung naked and swaying above the raging waters, raked too by machine-gun fire. Twenty volunteers pressed forward, armed with grenades. They swung their way, hand over hand, along the chains. The army watched in deathly silence. The first fell, struck by bullets. Then the second. Then the third. Then the fourth got through. Climbing on to the remaining planks, and with deadly aim, he landed his grenade among the guns.

Many other volunteers followed, and, despite the flames from the paraffin-soaked remaining planks, poured over to the attack. A loud roar of "Long live the Red Army," "Long live the heroes of the Tatu Ho," rose, as fresh streams of volunteers poured across the river, extinguishing the flames and replacing the planks. Chiang's troops had already fled, only to be met with cross-fire from the Red Army detachment on the northern bank, who had outpaced Chiang's troops and arrived first at the northern end of the crossing.

In an hour or two the whole army was marching joyously across the river into the Szechuan Province.

The next obstacle was the 16,000-foot high Snowy Mountain, with all the terror of snow and rarefied air for southerners, straight from the hot lowlands and clad only in light cotton suits. The suffering was intense. The 90,000 troops had dwindled to 40,000, though some army men had remained as partisans to harass the rear of the White armies.

After the Snowy Mountain came the hostile Mantus and the deserted grasslands. Ten days without sight of habitation or trees. Perilous swamps on every hand. Soaking rain. No timber. No fires. No cooked food. Many sank out of sight and were drowned in the swamps. The grasslands at least shook off the White Army pursuers. The Red Army got through, but with numbers reduced to 20,000.

At phenomenal speed the Army had traveled: an average over all this difficult terrain and through heavy fighting of twenty-four miles a day for a year. Covering 7,000 miles of march, crossing eighteen mountain ranges and twenty-four rivers, and breaking through enveloping armies of warlords in ten different provinces.

But what an advertisement, what a propaganda march! For what looked like a defeat and a strategic retreat had been turned into a masterly triumphal procession and advance. The fame of the People's Liberation Army spread along the whole mileage of the March through ten provinces. The disciplined life, the helpfulness, the consideration for poor peasants left not only a trail of hope behind, but the glow of a new morality, destined to affect profoundly the future of an independent and unified China.

The Long March was propaganda of the highest order, brilliant not only as a piece of consummately skilled military strategy, but as a piece of skilled political strategy equally consummate. The Red Army March will stand high in military history and high in political history. It is the contrasting counterpart to Napoleon's Retreat from Moscow. There the Grand Army retreated through thousands of miles utterly broken and demoralized. The Chinese strategic retreat grew into a triumphal march, consummating itself after strenuous and successful combat against Japanese aggression and Kuomintang treachery, in the mighty army of five million strong, as it is today.

And who were these men who had struggled so valiantly through so much adversity? The vanguard of the Red Army were not bandits, nor outlaws, nor malcontents. They were young peasants and workers who believed they were fighting for their homes, their land, their country. Their average age was nineteen, many had enlisted at sixteen, more than half were peasants. Only 4 percent petty bourgeois and intellectuals. It was a steeled force which emerged from the March.

Unlike the White troops, 60 to 70 percent of these youths were literate, coming as they did from the areas organized as revolutionary bases. They received no pay. Most were unmarried. Few drank or smoked. Drunkenness was unknown. Extreme youth, constant exertions and hardships, and adventure made the lack of feminine companionship endurable. Able to march twenty-four miles a day, they were the swiftest army in the world. Solid, disciplined, knowing what they wanted and why they fought, they were as invincible as Cromwell's Ironsides.

The Red Army was a national army, enlisted from all areas. Men and officers dressed largely alike, lived alike, and ate alike.

The victorious Long March was concluded, and the Red Army had arrived in Shensi at the psychologically right moment. It marked the turning point from danger to safety for the Chinese Revolution. It gave the Chinese people hope for the future and confidence in the success of the anti-Japanese movement. It convinced China of the invincible strength of the Communist Party and the Red Army. It forced China to see that she must rely upon the Communist Party to put an end to the insatiable encroachments of Japan.

China saw that civil war against the Communists must cease. The voice of the people was growing. And it grew louder and louder as Japan invaded farther and farther, and launched advanced attacks throughout the whole of northern China. The students of Peking began a "Resist Japan and Save China Movement" on December fifth, 1935. It spread to the whole country. The broad masses of the people were swept in and took up the Communist Party slogan: "Stop civil war; unite to resist Japan." The tide of revolution had risen once again.

With wisdom, Mao met the advance. He saw the problem. He perceived that if it was to be a united China movement, it must have room for petty bourgeoisie and national bourgeoisie, as well as for workers and peasants. The title People's Republic replaced that of Workers' and Peasants' Republic. The property of the anti-imperialist national bourgeoisie was to be protected. Only a united national army could smash Japanese aggression.

THE WAR OF RESISTANCE—LIBERATION

In 1936, when the Long March had ended in the triumphal entry into Shensi Province, the Communist Party sent an open appeal to the Kuomintang to end civil war and concentrate all forces on repelling the Japanese aggression.

Chiang stubbornly resisted the Communist proposals, but was dramatically arrested at Sian by his own generals, Chang Hsueh-liang and Yang Hu-cheng, on his way to attack the Red Army. Extracting a promise that he would turn his army against the Japanese and at Chou En-lai's own request, Chiang Kai-shek was released. The civil war ended. Peace within the country was restored. The Chinese people recognized in the plans of the Communist Party the only chance of deliverance from the Japanese menace.

Japan renewed her attacks in 1937. Reorganized as the Eighth Route Army and the New Fourth Army, the Communist forces moved to the front and the united War of Resistance began.

Mao outlined the probable course of events; resistance would be long-drawn-out; final victory would be won in three stages: withdrawal, stalemate, and then the Chinese offensive. Guerrilla warfare would be practiced at once in the enemy's rear. Mobile warfare when conditions were favorable. The Kuomintang would grow weaker, the Communist Party and People's Liberation Army stronger. With an international anti-fascist front, the balance of power would be reversed. Eight years of war proved Mao's analysis to be correct. The Kuomintang had grown weaker. The Communist Party had grown stronger.

The Japanese occupied Wuhan in October, 1938. Further advance was halted by the Eighth Route Army and the New Fourth Army on the northwest front. Angrily, the Japanese turned to "mop up" the Communist forces, applying the policy "Burn all, kill all, loot all." Chiang Kai-shek aided the Japanese by treacherously launching in 1940 and 1943 three vigorous anti-Communist campaigns. Blockading the liberated areas, he instructed his forces in the enemy's rear to surrender and join the Japanese against the Communists.

The result was twofold. On the one hand, the liberated areas for a while shrank in size. But on the other hand the masses, in the rear of the Japanese, formed People's Militia with armed civilians' work-teams to harass the Japanese rear.

The Communist forces put up a terrific fight. Short of material, save what they took from the enemy, short of medical stores, they yet fought on. They consolidated the liberated areas, raised the quality of the fighting troops, simplified the government administration, laying incidentally the foundation for the New China.

From 1943 onward the two Communist armies were able to switch over from guerrilla war to mobile war, to launch local attacks, to extend the liberated areas, to invest important cities and traffic lines. By the time the Russian Soviet Army had declared war against Japan in 1945, the popular forces had grown to 1,280,000 strong. Then, while the Russian troops annihilated the cream of the Japanese forces and liberated the northwest, the Communist armies wiped out large numbers of Japanese and puppet troops on the fronts they faced.

These victories completely upset Chiang Kai-shek's calculations. He reckoned that the Communist forces, placed in the forefront of the battle and attacked by his forces in the rear and by the Japanese in front, would have been exterminated during the War of Resistance. To that end he had avoided battle and husbanded his forces. Instead, the Communist forces had grown in number and quality. Henceforth it was a race as to which side would enter first into the vacuum caused by the Japanese collapse.

Chiang was backed by the limitless financial and transport resources of the U.S.A., whose airplanes transported one million of his men to the north. By starting this large-scale counter-revolutionary war in 1946, Chiang set off China's Third Revolutionary War, despite the efforts which the Communist Party had made for peace, democracy, and unity in August, 1945.

The United States-equipped Kuomintang Army of 4,300,000 men, twice the size of the People's forces, had control of China's major cities, and most of her railways. But it fared no better than it did in Chiang's mass attacks in Kiangsi of earlier years. Under Mao's guidance the Communist forces withdrew from various regions and exterminated the enemy piecemeal by concentrating superior forces at strategic points in mobile warfare. After eight months, 700,000 of Chiang's forces were wiped out. After February, 1947, Chiang launched an offensive at certain key points.

At the close of the same year one million Kuomintang troops were out of action. The People's Army had grown to two million. The Kuomintang offensive was smashed. The Liberation Army took over the offensive.

The change was basic and dramatic. The Liberation Army had expanded in number. Equipped with captured U.S. arms, big Liberation Army corps moved up with heavy artillery to attack the Kuomintang at strategic points. Between September, 1948, and January, 1949, the Liberation Army had launched eight major campaigns from Mukden and Tientsin down to Huaihai, near Pengpu on the Huai River, putting 1,540,000 Kuomintang troops out of action. Nanking fell on April 23, 1949. Huge armies in the southwest, south, and northwest of China collapsed. Four million Kuomintang troops had been scattered. The rule of Chiang Kai-shek had ended. The era of feudalism, imperialism, and bureaucratic capitalism had ended with it.

In October, 1949, the Central People's Government of the People's Republic of China was founded, with Mao Tse-tung as Chairman.

The Common Program of the new Government outlines its general principles:

"The People's Republic of China is a New Democratic or a People's Democratic state. It carries out the people's democratic dictatorship led by the working class, based on the alliance of workers and peasants and uniting all democratic classes and all nationalities in China. It opposes imperialism, feudalism, and bureaucratic capitalism and strives for the independence, democracy, peace, unity, prosperity, and strength of China."

3 Is Marxism Applicable to China?

"MARXISM and Leninism are inapplicable to China's life and conditions." We have often heard the assertion. It is baseless. So too is the kindred assertion that "China cannot have a class war because 'China has no classes,' only varying degrees of poverty."

"In that respect," so the assertion proceeds, "China differs from Russia. Therefore China's brand of communism must differ too. The Chinese are essentially individualist: Socialism and communism can never thrive in China. China needed neither a class struggle against feudalism nor a national struggle against imperialism. All she needed was 'compromise,' 'friendship' between the landlords and peasants, and 'co-existence' and 'co-prosperity' between the Chinese people and the imperialist powers."

That also is not true, and never has been true. Peasant struggles have torn Chinese society for 2,000 years and anti-imperialist struggles have continued ever since the Opium War a century ago. So long as 95 percent of the rural population occupied only 40 percent of the land there was bound to be class struggle, heroic class struggle, side by side with national struggle for national independence. Class struggle has been the motive for the development of Chinese society, precisely as it was the motive force for the struggle and development in Russia and in all other countries.

Class struggle has already achieved the liquidation of bureaucratic capitalism, just as the national struggle has ended imperialist rule. A semi-colonial China has become an independent China and a semi-feudal China has become a new democratic China.

"Why then," it is asked, "does the Chinese Communist Party co-operate with the national bourgeoisie, whereas Stalin and the Russian Communist Party entirely liquidated Russian capitalism?"

The answer is simple. The conditions in both countries have differed. The goal in both is the same. The path to the goal has differed because the conditions differed. The matter must be viewed in each country according to the actual conditions existing there at the time. Russia had her own historical conditions; China hers. China was a semi-feudal and semi-colonial country. Her revolution sought to overthrow both feudalism and imperialism. And when bureaucratic capitalism arose and also became counter-revolutionary, as it did, the revolution sought to overthrow that too.

That meant that the revolution must be led by the workers and peasants. It was a revolution against imperialism, feudalism, and bureaucratic capitalism. Such a revolution in its early stages need not hurt the national-bourgeoisie at all, and as a matter of fact did not hurt them. Indeed, it brought, as we see, more grist to their mill. At certain stages in the Chinese revolution—for instance, during the anti-Japanese war and during the war of Liberation against Chiang Kai-shek and the Americans which followed it—a certain section of the national bourgeoisie co-operated with the Communists and the democratic people. This was fully consistent with Marxism. Did not Marx and Engels say in *The Communist Manifesto* that the Communists "fight with the bourgeoisie whenever it acts in a revolutionary way, against the absolute monarchy, or the feudal squirearchy"? Stalin in the Second World War did the same; he co-operated with capitalist England and America against fascist Germany.

It is an important principle. A concrete analysis must always be applied to a concrete situation. Constant observance of that principle was the strength of Mao Tse-tung. The policy he adopted in one stage differed from the policy he adopted in another. Decisions, he urged, and rightly urged, must never be made according to subjective doctrine or based on limited experience.

This principle revealed the two-faced character of the Chinese national bourgeoisie and so implied a twofold tactical procedure on the part of the Chinese Communist Party and the proletariat. The Chinese national bourgeoisie tended, as a capitalist class, to struggle against the proletariat; it was forced also by self-interest to struggle with the proletariat against all aggression and against the all-absorbing Japanese and other kindred imperialists. So too the proletariat had at one time to struggle against the national bourgeoisie and at another time to struggle with it. The truth of Marxism-Leninism concerning the reality of the class struggle was constant. Mao Tse-tung integrated it in this perfectly logical way in his concrete practice.

Naturally Mao Tse-tung met with opposition in his own party. There were purists who said, "Never join with the national bourgeoisie on any account; stick to the task of eliminating the feudal landlords and the big anti-national capitalists and the national capitalists with them. Eliminate all the capitalists." But this was impossible while Japan was battering at the door, seeking to crush the Chinese proletariat and swallow at the same time the Chinese national capitalists. To join with the national capitalists against the common foe first was obviously the correct policy: settle sectional differences afterward. Precisely that principle impelled the national bourgeoisie to co-operate with the Communists against Japan. It was at that stage a matter of mutual interest to co-operate.

The fundamental principle of Chinese communism, however, has never changed. It is actuated by precisely the same principle as Russian communism, and all Eastern European communism, as indeed of all communism. The temporary modes of operation differ because the conditions differ. At the present stage the Communist Party and the people are fighting for the realization of the new democracy in China. Its final aim is to realize the system of communism in all its fullness in China.

Again, it was urged that a so-called Communist Party, with 80 percent of its members peasants or of peasant origin—since the Party in the early days of the first Revolutionary War had been obliged to leave the towns and build up bases in the country—could never, with a peasant mind and peasant experience, be 100 percent communist. Such a party, some urged, could never introduce real communism into China or even lay sound foundations for it.

They were wrong. First we may notice that many socialist world leaders were peasants or small-scale capitalists. Secondly, Party members of peasant origin, just like industrial worker members, were educated in the teachings of Lenin and Stalin. Party members also followed a strict collective life and organizational discipline with a correct communist outlook. Thirdly, the Party had trained large numbers of leaders, who had grown up, in long-drawn-out struggles, to a high level of political consciousness. These new leaders had rid themselves of the limitations and tendencies derived from small holdings and small-scale production. Fourthly, the peasant members were drawn from the poor, not the rich peasant class; they were in the main semi-proletarians of the countryside. More than 30 percent had indeed long left the countryside. Many had served as officers in the People's Liberation Army—living, that is, in a revolutionary military organization, the "supply system" of military communism. To most of them, their peasant origin was merely a factor of their past. The number of people who had lived under this communist system, this "supply system"—living, that is, a strictly collective life—had grown from tens of thousands to hundreds of thousands, By 1951 they had grown to eight million, more than double the number of industrial workers in the factories of China.

4 China's New Morality

"OUR deepest impressions sprang from no great physical achievements, no constructive works built in record time. They sprang from the astonishingly great moral change in the new China of today."

I quote the words of a near relative, a missionary doctor of nine years' standing, who, with her husband, also a doctor, served in the Liberation Government employment a final year before their return to England after their hospital had been taken over by the State.

The moral change outweighed all other factors and lay at the root of all China's great successes. Moral change which penetrated deep into the lives of the common people. Observable in great matters vital to all, such as flood protection. Observable also in the intimate personal life of individuals, as in the case of children and pregnant women.

As medical workers, my kinfolk saw the mass attack on ill health in

Led to execution --- His only crime an effort to organise the workers.

field and factory and the unbelievable new attitude to the aged, the sick and to timid juvenile workers.

It may, and doubtless will, take long for this spirit to permeate the whole of China. But the leaven is there and daily at work and the range of Chinese activities already affected is great.

In the China of 1932, as I knew it, to take a stark illustration, a man lay wounded in the street. Nobody dared to touch him. An American lady started forward to help, wishing to summon an ambulance. "Don't touch him," said her companion. "You'll be responsible for paying the ambulance and hospital. If he dies, you will be responsible for his funeral. If he lives as a cripple, you will be responsible for his maintenance."

That is an exaggerated picture of what was still very generally true of the old China. It could not happen today. It is the center of gravity which has changed. The moral character of the Government has changed, and the change travels right down the line. The Government cares for the individual and welcomes all aid given to the individual.

This chapter will deal with the positive moral achievements of the new Liberation Government and the new spirit among the people. Doubtless, dark spots remain. It could hardly be otherwise in a country twice the size of Europe, with three times the population. These dark spots have been deliberately exaggerated, especially in connection with the Red Army, against which a daily flood of false propaganda has poured out for years. According to the Western press, the Red Army moved as a pestilence amongst the harmless Chinese.

But even in 1932 there were other witnesses. Red Army men, for instance, were billeted in the home of two maiden ladies, missionary relatives of mine. The men, they told me, behaved in every way correctly.

Major Todd, the American engineer with whom I traveled to Inner Mongolia and Tibet, spoke strongly of the difference of government in the Communist areas from that in the Kuomintang areas. But stories of Red brutality still deluged the press.

Rewi Alley gives an excellent example of the genesis of these anti-Communist stories. Making an inspection at Juichin in Kiangsi, a young official of the Kuomintang was deputed to accompany him. Pointing to some old ruins, the official said: "See what the Reds did." Alley turned to a nearby peasant and asked, "How did that school come to be burned?" The peasant replied: "The Red Army had a school there; the Nanking troops bombed it to the ground." The official scowled.

Again, to give just one other example, a German missionary named Engel and an American named Johnson were constant sources of evil stories. One day Engel said: "The Communists had a printing press here where they printed banknotes. When they left they took all the printers and the machines out there," pointing vaguely to the hills. "They made the printers bury the machines and then shot them."

"Come, come, Mr. Engel," said Rewi Alley. "We have just bought the old Red Army printing equipment, and there it is in our new co-operative. As for the people, all the members of our new Ningtu printing co-operative were once working in the banknote printing works here." Engel carried his tales elsewhere.

Of the brutality of the Kuomintang, on the other hand, there is abundant evidence. I need not be told of the Kuomintang general at Changsha saying frankly and proudly in the presence of Europeans, a friend of mine among them: "I drove the lot of them into the sewer to drown; without doubt there were Communists among them and if a few honest men were drowned as well, at any rate I got my man among them. I was thorough."

I was familiar with this attitude to life in 1932. I saw a man shot as he knelt down on the road with his hands tied behind his back: "Suspected Communist," I was told. I have a photograph of a gallant young worker, led to execution by two soldiers: his only crime an effort to organize the workers against atrocious factory conditions in Shanghai. Seldom have I seen so radiant a face. And I compare it with the exalted spirit of the bobbed-haired Chinese Communist student, saying, as she stood before the guns of the executioners, "You are living for a little thing. I am dying for a big thing. I would rather die for a big thing than live for a little thing."

Turn, however, now to the positive achievements of the new morality.

THE MASS ATTACK ON POVERTY

Rewi Alley, who has lived for long years under the shadow of Chinese poverty, recalls a visit to the Red Stone Lake. "The last time we went," he writes, "the farmer in his bare living-room preserved the empty ration can we had given him the year before. On the *k'ang* lay his wife and several children, all sick; over them his tattered sheepskin coat. He himself was going about in a daze, crying a little from red-rimmed eyes, desperate to know what to do about them. In the house nothing. Bandits had taken his animals. Passing soldiers had stolen the felt from his *k'ang*. Just a peasant and his family, sick in mind and body—yet representing that vast mass of peasantry throughout Asia, wanting, demanding something better than this."

All that hopeless, helpless peasant poverty has gone, driven hence by the action of the new morality in high places which not only made an end of banditry and corrupt soldiery, and freed the peasant from feudal landlordism, but provided for the poverty-stricken peasant a means of escape from physical catastrophe. For the new morality has shown up brilliantly in tackling floods and droughts, the main physical cause of Chinese poverty.

No basic solution of China's flood problems had ever been attempted. Officials had imposed and collected taxes here and there, but no radical and comprehensive work was undertaken, and the money in bulk seldom went to flood prevention. The people were left to pitiable destruction.

The loss caused by flood was colossal—not only direct loss through drowning, but indirect loss through starvation. Flood over a large area meant death by starvation for millions and economic ruin for many more unless outside help was rushed in, a thing seldom attempted and, owing to lack of transport, seldom possible.

In the recent flood in the Huai River, five million tons of grain were lost. Death seemed imminent till the new morality stepped in to stay it. Wheat and millet were rushed from Manchuria by train and canal, and the peril passed, and major operations for water control began forthwith.

The immorality of man had been a major factor in China's flood problems. For thousands of years the Huai River had flowed smoothly down its channel to the sea, until the Chins, pressed by Genghis Khan from the north, allowed the Yellow River to burst its banks, causing havoc to the Huai River, silting its bed and shifting its course. For 700 years the Yellow River flowed into the sea via the Huai and the Yangtze, and then left the bed it had silted and once more returned to its old channel northward.

There it remained till Chiang Kai-shek, to save his soldiery for the struggle against the Liberation Army, blew up its banks and flooded vast areas in an attack upon the Japanese, utterly regardless of a catastrophe to his own people which cost half a million lives through drowning and millions more through man-made famine.

Once again the Yellow River was diverted by Chiang Kai-shek to cut in two the Communist areas, again regardless of the misery it caused.

Reckless disregard of human life marked the Kuomintang, and neither they nor their predecessors had ever felt the moral urge to cure an age-old menace.

The Liberation leaders felt the urge, and sought and found the remedy. For the first time in history a radical scheme for the radical solution of the flood problem was sought and found. Already the success has been great and we no longer read of Chinese millions dying of hunger.

The same large-scale moral action, looking toward the far future, plants forests and forest belts to guard the land from dessicating winds, giving promise of change of climate and abundant harvests.

THE NEW MORALITY IN INDUSTRY

Life in the Kuomintang factory was even worse than life on the Kuomintang farm. Horrible at the dawn of life, it was horrible through each hopeless subsequent stage. As a factory inspector in Shanghai under the Kuomintang, Rewi Alley's whole being could stand it no longer, and, hastening away, he began that series of co-operative enterprises which make a golden chapter in China's life and foreshadowed the spirit of the new Liberation days.

Alley speaks, for example, of the nightmarish silk filature factories of Shanghai, with their long line of children, many not more than eight or nine years old, standing for twelve hours a day over boiling vats of cocoons, with swollen red fingers, eyes inflamed, eye muscles sagging, many crying from the beating of the foreman, who walked up and down behind them with a piece of No. 8 gauge wire as a whip; with tiny arms often scalded in punishment if they passed a thread incorrectly, in rooms so full of steam that standing in them for a few minutes was unbearable. I had heard of these things. Alley saw them.

Child accidents were appalling. Of one batch of orphans sent by the Child Welfare Association to toil at the factory as small orphan children were sent in early industrial British days to the workhouse to toil in British factories, practically all had received injuries from the fast-running, unguarded presses. Out of some sixty-four children working at one time over thirty had fingers or portions of fingers missing.

That nightmare is gone. All gone. Child labor in Chinese factories is forbidden by law.

Pass to the adolescent child, the growing youth. Alley speaks of beriberi in the factory, of lads with legs swollen twice their normal size. In the smaller factories almost all the boy workers were affected. Dull, listless, and apathetic, they would work till they could work no longer. A diet of polished rice and old cabbage, lack of ventilation, work for twelve to fourteen hours a day, and general hopelessness had robbed them of any chance of health. Let me quote this most moving passage:

"Once I packed a car full of the worst sufferers from one of the factories and took them to a hospital. . . . We went up in the hospital lift and their apathetic eyes took light and a little life. One of them looked up at me and from his pocket took out two tiny electric flashlight bulbs, one red and one blue, and pushed them from his sweating hands into mine. 'Good to play with,' he said. They were his only possessions and I could not offend by not taking them. They stayed with me on my desk for years, a reminder of the struggle of one small life against the rotten world of his day."

Alley's final disillusionment about any possibility of reform in the old regime came when he saw a group of lads, who had been organizing silk filature workers, executed as "Communists" for that crime. They were carried to the execution ground suspended from poles, half-naked and well roped up, and there thrown to the ground. A Kuomintang officer walked up to each and blew his brains out with a pistol shot; a fat boy in silk cap and gown standing by clapping his hands in excitement and joy.

That nightmare too is gone—all gone. Just as no small child is allowed by the new morality to work in a Chinese factory, so no adolescent is allowed to overwork. No worker is allowed to suffer as the beri-beri boys suffered. Article 7 of the Trade Union Law underlines the duty of the management of any factory to protect the interests of workers and staff in the matter of labor protection, labor insurance, factory sanitation, safety measures, and all other measures for improving the cultural life of the workers. Textile factories are to be air-conditioned. Water sprays to keep down the dust, ventilation, and adequate light are a first charge on factory administration.

No more vivid contrast to the capitalist factories of Alley's day could be imagined than the jute factory I saw at Hangchow, with its fine workshops, noble cultural rooms, glowing gardens, and comely hostels for the workers.

AGRARIAN REFORM

The Chinese way of carrying out reforms also feels the impact of the new morality.

The division of the land among the tillers of the land was a mighty moral act; the more so as all too often the landlord had on one pretext or another wrongfully gained the land.

But no less moral was the mercy mingled with justice meted out to the landlords at the land division and after.

The Agrarian Reform Law of 1950 reflects the political maturity of the Chinese leaders in insuring that no injustice shall be done to any section of the community, neither to dispossessed landlords, depriving them of all means of livelihood, nor even to those who have bitterly opposed progress in the past. A total of up to one percent of the land in any area is set aside for landlords or other guilty people who fled or worked with the enemy. If they have not committed any war crimes, they will get land when they return to the village. Priests, monks, and nuns will also be given land on the same basis as other members of the community if they have no other source of income. Land bought with the earnings of the owner's own labor, or belonging to old people living alone, helpless widows or widowers who depend on the income from rent for their livelihood, is to remain their property.

HONESTY

A nation-wide movement to introduce a high moral tone among officials in Government employment on the one hand, and workers and staffs in capitalist enterprises on the other hand, led in the first half of the year 1952 to a twofold campaign, known respectively as the *san fan* and the *wu fan* campaigns.

The *san fan* movement was aimed against corruption, waste, and bureaucracy among Government employees, the *wu fan* movement against bribery, tax evasion, theft of State property, cheating on Government contracts, and stealing economic information from Government sources for private speculation.

The percentage of government employees found guilty of corruption was four to five percent. The most serious cases were sent to the courts for trial. Discipline and working efficiency have increased: Government expenditure has been reduced.

It was otherwise with the *wu fan* movement, where it touched 450,000 private, industrial, and commercial establishments in nine major cities, like Shanghai, Canton, and Hankow. Of these 76 percent were found guilty of various illegal transactions. Here again the most serious cases were tried in the courts, the remainder dealt with along the lines of re-education.

The effect already has been highly promising. It shows itself in many ways. A new honesty confronts one in diverse and unexpected places. The railway bookstall, for instance, on the Peking Station or the children's bookstall in Shanghai have books arranged and prices fixed, but no attendant to receive the payment, only a box for coins. Yet generally there is more, not less, in the box than required to balance the purchases.

The poet Lao Sheh told us that he took some friends to lunch at a café and ordered a cattie bottle of wine. They brought two bottles, a cattie bottle and another much smaller. The so-called cattie bottle was below standard; the smaller bottle supplied the deficit.

SELF-CRITICISM

Self-criticism is a new and important element in the new morality. An intriguing element too, almost unheard of in the West, where the ruling tone is self-justification and self-exaltation. What businessman of the West criticizes himself? He belauds himself. His soap washes cleanest, his toothpaste makes teeth whiter, his aspirin gives sounder sleep. Doctors in the West are largely exempt from criticism; judges too; and the parson trusts to the protection of the pulpit.

But criticism becomes customary in China. To encounter it produces at first a shock of unreality. In a long talk with a professor in a southern Chinese university, I learned that only after great struggle and fierce self-criticism had he been reformed, re-educated, refashioned, in the new way of collective thinking, though he knew he had a long way yet to go.

He was a quiet, thoughtful man, immersed in his professional tasks. Thoroughly satisfied with the old feudalistic order, he lived his own individual, isolated life.

The first step in his new education began when the new Government sent out a radio warning that a typhoon was approaching and urged every individual citizen to "make everything secure." The professor thought this was mere scare and wondered why. Then the typhoon broke. Owing to the warning and instant action, very little damage was done. But the incident awakened him. Such warnings had never come over the air before. Why this new thought of the collective for the individual, for each individual?

So he started to think. Then he began to criticize his own way of life, his own actions and outlook. What was his own attitude to the collective and to individuals? These were the early steps in his re-education. Not yet, he asserted with humility, was he fully changed. He had come a long way; he was sure he had further to go: but he was pressing on, entering a new world.

Criticism and self-criticism is the lifeblood of the new order. "Am I living my life to the best advantage?" "Am I working well and efficiently?" "Can other members of the collective or the community help me to a nobler spirit and more efficient service?" This seems fantastic to the West; less so when immersed in the practice of criticism and self-criticism in the East.

We ourselves practiced self-criticism as a team in our rail journey through China. Midway in our intensive travel, our guides and organizers proposed a mutual criticism meeting to overhaul our methods with a view to greater efficiency. Had we used our precious time to the best advantage? Had we wasted opportunities of study? We met in our dining salon: the leader, the organizer, the doctor, our two guides, and others. We put all cards on the table, suggesting improved modes of work and saying where we felt we had collectively or individually failed.

We for our part suggested, for example, that when visiting a factory, a place of work, or a place historically significant, our guides might gather beforehand the facts and figures for our information, preventing their constant repetition. Thus we would gain a compact picture of the situation and be free to ask salient questions and get intimate conversation with many more individuals. That suggestion, subsequently adopted, saved considerable time.

Mutual criticism and self-criticism is a widespread growth in present-day China. Ministers meet their congregations to discuss their sermons and the conduct of parish work. Intellectuals live with and help peasants during the business of land reform: daily living in a worker's cottage is itself a criticism. The intellectual is shocked when he recognizes the cost of his education in relation to the earnings of a peasant family, each year of his education costing the combined income of a dozen or so of these poor, toiling peasants.

The positive effect of these self-examinations is frequently astonishing. A doctor in a lucrative post, friend of our own accompanying doctor, was offered a post in a distant and uncultured place with a fraction of the pay he had been receiving. Because he now felt the need of the people so strongly and because he had learned that there was a dearth of doctors in the distant post, with a comparative plenty in Peking, he went on the new mission without a word. He had been well trained in the social re-orientation of his mind.

Peter Townsend, in one of a series of article in *The New Statesman and Nation,* gives his own experience as a worker in a co-operative under the new regime:

"It happened that a quarrel, a stupid clash of personalities, was upsetting the office routine. Two responsible staff members were involved. One thought the other was after his job. The second felt he was being ignored and pushed into the background. Both had once been in business, and both were university graduates. One morning it was suggested that the work of the office should be taken as the topic and that each one should describe his part, how he did it, what difficulties he encountered, and what he felt were his deficiencies in his job. The consensus was that the time for it was overripe, and the one Communist in the group (which also included an ex-Communist) agreed to start the ball rolling by appraising his own activities. The following morning he began by making an astonishingly frank assessment of his shortcomings, which others added to. . . . There was a pause. The contestants were obviously called upon to speak, though no one expressly said so. One excused himself, saying he would like to think his action over. The other began, very slowly, to disclose his own feelings on the conflict which held up the organization's work. The matter was not cleared up for several days, by which time everyone had discussed his or her own work. Half-disclosures were followed by general discussion, general discussion by greater frankness. These two contestants, after all, were 'bosses' who had criticized and never before been criticized. They had to overcome pride, conceit, and the fear that acknowledging their mistakes might lower their prestige and authority, and the way they responded emphasized the hesitations and pride of the intellectuals."

Here surely is a story reminiscent of the primitive Christian professions of a humble and contrite heart, and also the story of the communal forgiveness of the early Christian communities. In a modern industrial nation, such as China is becoming, however, such an outlook, permeating to the many millions as yet untouched, gives promise of unimaginable moral strength side by side with the new industrial strength. The center of Asia may well become a bastion of the best in human nature.

SOURCE OF THE NEW MORALITY

Whence came this mighty moral change? Naturally enough, it sprang, in the main, from the example of the whole-hearted self-sacrifice of the creative spirits who fashioned the new China and in the self-sacrificing labor of the People's Liberation Army, modeled deliberately on the moral outlook of the leaders, sealed too with the blood of countless martyrs in the liberation cause.

The answer to the call to build up a society so economically rich that it could "give to each according to need," so morally transformed that it dared to do so and willed to do so, had been as great in China as in the Western world. And it moved in the same direction. It was that which called forth, in both lands, men and women of the same type. A new moral type. The type demanded by the great moralists of all ages. The type demanded pre-eminently by Christianity. The type outlined when the Founder of Christianity enunciated the standard by which life, individual or national, will be tested. It was not, in his view, primarily by building churches or worshiping in them, not even by professed belief in God or regular practice of prayer. A man measures up to that standard by *action;* by *humane action,* by a right attitude to brother man. "Not every one that saith unto me, Lord, Lord, shall enter into the kingdom of heaven, but he that *doeth* the will of My Father which is in heaven." The *doing* and the *right doing* is the test: "I was hungry, what did you *do* about that? . . . Naked, sick, fettered and bound. What did you *do* about that?" There is the standard. Man's attitude to brother man is the standard. And surely it is demonstrably akin to the communist standard of "To each according to his need. From each according to his ability."*

Apply that standard to the present rulers of China. They stand high.

Mao Tse-tung, fitting himself from youth up to serve his country; living in voluntary austerity, even as a boy at school, compounding with school friends to talk only of high things, discarding talk of money, sex, or family affairs; seeking to know and understand the world around him; tramping deliberately penniless on holidays through the countryside to understand how men lived; refusing the path of lucrative employment, choosing rather to live dangerously and penuriously and work toward the moral and physical regeneration of China; putting the people's interest before his own self-interest; charging, single-handed, full tilt against the power of landlords, warlords, imperialists, compradores, and Chiang Kai-shek himself; building up a movement among the peasants which could raise them from penury and misery to affluence and culture; with a price as he endeavored to do so of a quarter of a million dollars on his head, and the same upon the heads of his distinguished comrades. If you seek

* Note carefully in this connection the parable of the talents—from each according to his ability—and the parable of the laborers in the vineyard—to each according to his need.

the cause of China's new morality, look there, look to Mao Tse-tung, look to Chu Teh, to Chou En-lai, to Kuo Mo-jo.

It is in these men, and tens of thousands more like them, in the multitudes of men and women who gave up their lives and met their death in the same cause, that we find the secret of the new moral order in China.

In these men and in the great Liberation Army, their instrument, which they had fashioned for achieving their goal, for overthrowing a regime that was immoral, cruel, and corrupt, for ejecting an imperialism which battened on the riches of colonial lands, hindering its inhabitants from achieving an all-round economy and ample living for themselves; an instrument for overthrowing a capitalism which put self and profit before brother man and society, an instrument inspired from first to last with the will to serve the people—it is there that we must look if we would find the source of the new widespread morality.

Study carefully the concrete rules, so strictly observed by the Liberation Army soldier under the guidance of his steeled leaders.

1. Obey orders under all circumstances.
2. Do not take a single needle or piece of thread from the people.
3. Hand in all enemy booty to the Government.

Study the many specific points signaled out for close attention:

1. Replace all doors (used as beds) when you leave a house.
2. Return or roll up the straw matting on which you sleep.
3. Be courteous and polite to the people and help them when you can.
4. Return all borrowed articles and replace all damaged goods.
5. Be honest in all transactions with the peasants.
6. Pay for all articles purchased.
7. Do not damage crops.
8. Do not beat or scold the people.
9. Do not behave unseemly with women.
10. Be sanitary.
11. Do not ill-treat prisoners of war.

Drilled in the discipline of the Long March, practicing these rules through ten provinces, leaving behind them a trail of good will and good example, expanding in the long struggle until reaching five million men, a source of moral strength among the people. Do we wonder at the change in the moral tone of Chinese society? Some by fear, some by admiration and emulation, the whole is leavened.

It is in the spirit of China's liberation leaders, instilled by them into the Red Army they had created and passed over by that Army to the mass of the peasantry, that we must seek and shall find the main source of China's new morality.

Hitherto, however, and right up to modern times, the practice of "giving according to need" has been hindered by the physical impossibility of acting up to the precept, and the precept has been allowed to fall into abeyance. Part of the new order in China, Russia, and Eastern Europe is the knowledge that the means to do precisely this are now being brought into being. All that is required is the will and the organization, and that the new morality supplies.

"Organization," that favorite keyword in Mao's vocabulary, which sprang to his lips at the recital of former floods, droughts, and famine and brought moisture to his eyes: "They were not organized then." In Mao Tse-tung and his comrades the will is there, the means are ready to hand, and the conscious organization is achieved. Organization which is indeed the one constant feature of advance all along the evolutionary road, great and ever greater organization. Here in China, in Russia, in Eastern Europe is evolving greater and ever greater organization: therefore greater and ever greater power to "give to each according to need." The morality which seizes upon the power that science gives and uses it for the highest human aid, is morality of the highest order.

Today, in short, we have the means as well as the will to put into practice the new morality, the new ethical demands enunciated by all the world's religious and moral leaders. And the most significant thing about new creative China is the new morality which is its finest fruit.

It is indeed this new morality, combined with the new belief in science and organization, which gives outstanding élan to the movements of the new China, as it did and does to the new Russia. It is a movement which comes so opportunely in the East. The thing is morally right. It is scientifically correct. It is a summons to all that is best in man. It is the answering echo to the noblest utterances of men. And it is invincible. No massed attack of privilege can ever prevail against this great new thing. Those who assail it do so at their peril. It is a rock unshakable. Those who fall against it will be shattered in the fall. The toils and pains and sufferings which have ushered in the new world of the new morality are not the death pangs pictured by frustrated religionists: they are birth pangs—birth pangs of the new science, the new hope, the new joy, the new morality of the new creative China which moves now into a foremost, and her rightful, place among the nations in a world renewed.

APPENDIX

APPEALS OF CHINESE CHRISTIAN LEADERS FOR PEACE AND AGAINST THE USE OF GERM WARFARE BY AMERICAN FORCES IN KOREA

THE APPEAL OF THE CHINESE PROTESTANTS

CHINA, *June 28th, 1952*

DEAR DEAN AND MRS. JOHNSON:

You have been warmly welcome to New China as your arrival has symbolized that Chinese and English Christians are making united efforts to defend world peace.

We Christians of China would like to report to you an inhuman and anti-Christian crime recently committed by the American aggressors, which is the bacteriological warfare they have launched against the Chinese and the Korean people. Rev. Wong Tzu-chung of the Peking Congregational Church went to Korea and North-East China as a representative of the Chinese religious circles and saw with his own eyes the various germ-laden insects dropped by the U.S. armed forces as well as shells of containers carrying insects. He collected with his own hands a great many evidences of the American bacteriological warfare. Many of our Christian doctors have witnessed the germ-disseminating insects and other carriers spread by the American aggressive forces, and taken active part in making every effort to defeat the American bacteriological warfare. We Chinese Christians confirm that the crimes of the bacteriological warfare committed by the American aggressors are irrefutable and undeniable.

Science should be used to cure people's disease, but the American aggressors are making use of it in spreading diseases, and evils will certainly be punished by God and condemned by the people of the whole world. We Chinese Christians should like to ask you to tell our fellow Christians of Britain and America and those elsewhere in the whole world about our strong protest against the United States of America for her crime of launching the bacteriological warfare. For the sake of humanity, righteousness and world peace, we want to appeal to the Christians throughout the world to raise protest so as to put a stop to the atrocious deeds of the American aggressors in massacring Chinese and Korean people with bacteriological weapons.

God be with you! Wishing you a bon voyage.

Respectfully yours,

Y. T. Wu, *Chairman, Christian Reform Committee.*
Liu Liang-mo, *Secretary, Christian Reform Committee.*
Robin Chen, *Presiding Bishop of the Anglican Church of China.*
P. C. Lin, *Secretary of the Anglican Church of China.*
Lindel Tsen, *Presiding Bishop of the Anglican Church of China* (retired).
Tseng Chien-neh, *General Secretary, Central Office Anglican Church of China.*
Lin Hsien-yang, *Bishop, North China and Shantung, Anglican Communion.*
H. H. Tsin, *General Secretary, Church of Christ in China.*
Tsai Chih-chung, *Secretary, Church of Christ in China.*
George Wu, *Chairman of National Christian Council of China.*
Hsieh Yung-ching, *Chairman, Chinese Independent Church.*
Chih Ching-tsai, *Chairman, China Baptist Council.*
Ai Nien-san, *Vice-Chairman, Lutheran Church.*
Mao Keh-chung, *Bishop of the Anglican Church.*
Chang Po-huai, *Secretary, Council of Christian Publishers.*
T. S. Yui, *Secretary, China Christian Endeavor Union.*
Z. T. Kaung, *Bishop, Methodist Church.*
Kiang Chung-kwang, *Vice-Chairman, Seventh Day Adventists.*
Ren Dah-ling, *Secretary, China Baptist Publication Society.*
K. Y. Yang, *Secretary, Chinese Home Missionary Society.*
Wu Chi-chung, *President, China Baptist Theological Seminary.*
Hsieh Shun-san, *Congregational Church.*
Peter Wang, *Chinese Independent Church.*
Cora Deng, *General Secretary, National Committee Y.W.C.A.*
Phoebe J. C. Shi, *Secretary, National Committee Y.W.C.A.*
Li Shou-bao, *Secretary, National Committee Y.M.C.A.*
K. H. Ting, *General Secretary, Christian Literature Society.*
Pong Tze-kun, *Chairman, Peking Church Federation.*
Chiang Yu-chang, *Acting President, School of Religion, Yenching University.*
Wang Chin-hsin, *Secretary, Methodist Church.*
Li Cheng-shen, *President, Peking Theological Seminary (Methodist).*
Wang Hua-ching, *Bishop (retired), Methodist Church.*
Lin Fang, *Major, Salvation Army, Peking.*

Ho Chin-te, *Brigadier, Salvation Army, Peking,*
and 376 other signatures of pastors and lay leaders of Protestant churches and organizations from Peking, Shanghai and Tientsin.

PEACE CALL OF HANCHOW CHRISTIAN LEADERS

HANCHOW, *June 13, 1952*

DEAR DR. JOHNSON:

Ever since we know your arrival in China we have been hoping that you will come to Hanchow. And now it has come true. We salute you most sincerely and respectfully as a progressive leader of the Christian Church and an outstanding fighter for peace. Herewith we present you a little souvenir to express our hearty welcome and sincere respect. We only regret that your visit to Hanchow was altogether too short.

Being believers of the Prince of Peace, we Christians in Hanchow, like Christians in other parts of the country, are ardent lovers of peace. We are now in the "Month for Defending World Peace" concentrating all our thoughts and prayers on this great movement. We realize that peace cannot be awaited, but must be won. We admire your rich life in the struggle for world peace, and your present visit is a great encouragement to us.

We love peace, therefore the more we hate the sin of killing the innocent. People of all countries long for a peaceful, happy life, and yet the warmongers are engaging in large-scale bacteriological warfare. Pastor T. C. Wong of Peking went to Korea to investigate himself and witnessed the facts of germ warfare. The sister-in-law of Rev. Shih Tien-ming of our city wrote back from Chichihar reporting that their city was attacked by germ warfare. Besides, there are the confessions of the captured American pilots, Enoch and Quinn. . . . All these facts have unmistakably told us that the American imperialists are launching a large-scale germ warfare against the Chinese and Korean people. This is not only a serious violation of international law, but also an abuse of human righteousness and human conscience. How can we Christians tolerate such criminal act, and to think of it coming from a country that claims to be "Christian."

We protest against the American imperialists' germ warfare. Many of our Christian medical workers throw themselves into the patriotic anti-pestilence campaign. We are prepared to devote all our strength to fight against germ warfare for the cause of world peace and the dignity of mankind. Meanwhile, we solemnly warn the handful of warmongers that tie up their fate with rats and fleas: Your days are numbered and your fate doomed.

Beloved Dean, we hope that you will disclose the facts of American imperialists' germ warfare to all peace-loving people of the world. They should no longer be deluded and threatened. Let us all have one faith, that is: Peace will win. Please tell the Christians in England that we Christians in new China have seen much clearer the light of the Gospel in the great revolutionary movement of people's liberation. May we shoulder up together the great task of defending world peace and peace will win greater victories when we meet again.

May God be with you always.

Your Brethren in Christ,

Kimber S. K. Deng, *Bishop of Chekiang Diocese, the Chinese Holy Catholic Church.*

Hsuen Shei-chiang, *Pastor of the Hu-San Church, the Church of Christ in China.*

T. C. Pao, *General Secretary, the Chekiang Shanghai Baptist Convention.*

Tsai Wen-hao, *General Secretary, Chekiang Synod of the Church of Christ in China.*

Fan Kwong-jong, *Pastor of the Sze-chen Church, the Church of Christ in China.*

Keng Tze-hua, *Pastor of the Ku-lou Church, the Church of Christ in China.*

Wu Chih-hsung, *Pastor of Chen-pei Church, the Church of Christ in China.*

King Chao-hsung, *Pastor of the Tai peng Church, the Church of Christ in China.*

Cheng Mien-yu, *Pastor of the Tien Shuei Church, the Church of Christ in China.*

Shih Tien-ming, *Pastor of Ming Chung Church.*

Chen Kwong-ying, *Pastor of Hanchow Church.*

Chang Liu-kwong, *Pastor of Chung Yi Church (China Inland Mission).*

Hsu Shih-hsun, *Pastor of the Seventh Day Adventists' Church.*

Tu Hao-shen, *Pastor of the Chen Shen Church.*

Wang Pi-teh, *Pastor of the Pentecostal Holiness Church.*

Yang Ja-keh, *Pastor, Jesus' Church.*

Niu Shu-chen, *Pastor of Lin Lien Church.*

Chen Siu-chen, *Pastor of the Lin Lien Church.*

Han Pi-teh, *Pastor of the Apostolic Faith Church.*

Chiu Chin-lin, *Dean, the China Theological Seminary.*

Wu Chih-hsung, *Dean, the Hanchow Bible Institute.*

Ke Chih-chan, *Pastor of the Chekiang Preaching Mission.*

Niu Chih-fong, *Hanchow Y.M.C.A.*

Chung Wen-chuen, *Hanchow Y.M.C.A.*

Chiu Chiu-lin, *Pastor of the Hu-San Church, the Church of Christ in China.*

LETTER FROM THE CHINESE CATHOLICS

PEKING, *June 30th, 1952*

DEAR DR. AND MRS. JOHNSON,

As peace-loving Chinese Catholics who love their country as well as their Church, we have raised strong protests with the anti-Christian bacteriological warfare waged by the American aggressors in Korea and China and have issued the "Manifesto issued by the Chinese Catholics Protesting Against the American Bacteriological Warfare". Up to now, the number of those who have signed on the Manifesto have amounted to 13,755, including two Bishops, two Coadjutor Bishops, 141 fathers, 130 priests, 110 nuns and 13,370 lay Catholics in different social circles. Signatures are still continuing to be gathered on a larger scale among Catholics of the whole country.

As you are the messenger for world peace, we now send you our Manifesto together with its English translation with the hope that you will tell all the Catholics of Britain, of the U.S.A. and of other countries in the world, about the protests of Chinese Catholics against the American bacteriological warfare, so that they may unite with us to stop the bacteriological warfare, waged by the American aggressors and to defend world peace.

Wishing you good health and bon voyage!

Chia Chen-ming, *Chairman of the Chinese Catholic Church Reform Committee of Peking.*

Li Chun-wu, *Assistant Bishop, the Peking Diocese, the Chinese Catholic Church.*

MANIFESTO OF CHINESE CATHOLICS

As free and fortunate Catholics of New China, we have in religious conscience raised strong protests with the American aggressors who have waged bacteriological warfare in Korea and China in violation of international conventions and against human morality.

The bacteriological warfare waged by the American aggressors has already been proved to be an irrefutable and ironclad fact through the investigations made by both Chinese and foreign people and through close examination by scientists. Here are two examples:

Rev. T. C. Wong of the Peking Congregational Church went as a representative of the Chinese religious circles to the Korean front and rear, as well as North-East China for the Investigation, heard with his own ears the accusations of the residents there, and saw with his own eyes the various germ-laden insects and containers carrying insects.

John Quinn and Kenneth L. Enoch, two P. O. Ws. of the U.S. Air

Force, confessed, out of the dictate of conscience, the guilt of how they had dropped germ bombs by direct order. Their expositions have proved that the germ warfare carried out by the American aggressors against the Chinese and Korean peoples is an action premeditated and carefully planned.

The American aggressors have called themselves "Christians", and alleged that they are "defending Christian civilization"; but in fact, the brutal crime of invading Korea committed by the American aggressors, especially the germ-warfare killing the peaceful residents of Korea and China, entirely violates Christian principles and morals, violates the Christian humanism and fraternity, and defiles the Peace Gospel of serving people preached by Christ.

As peace-loving Chinese Catholics who love their country as well as their Church, in the name of Christian principles and of Christian conscience, we protest against the American aggressors for their having carried out the bacteriological warfare. For the sake of dignity and righteousness of mankind, for the sake of the Gospel of Christ and for the sake of world peace, we stand for the prohibition of the use of bacteriological weapons. We appeal to the Catholics of the world and all the righteous and peace-loving people so as to unite together to stop the crimes of the American aggressors in waging the bacteriological warfare.

June 25, 1952

INDEX

www.ingramcontent.com/pod-product-compliance
Ingram Content Group UK Ltd.
Pitfield, Milton Keynes, MK11 3LW, UK
UKHW020819290926
15470UKWH00003B/1257